BLAZING TRAILS

COMING OF AGE IN
FOOTBALL'S GOLDEN ERA

JOHN MACKEY
WITH THOM LOVERRO

TRIUMPH
BOOKS
CHICAGO

Library of Congress Cataloging-in-Publication Data
Mackey, John, 1941–
    Blazing trails : coming of age in football's golden era / John Mackey with Thom Loverro.
        p. cm
    Includes index.
    ISBN 1-57243-538-0 (hard)
        1. Mackey, John, 1941– 2. Football players—United States—Biography. I. Loverro, Thom. II. Title.

GV939.M23A3 2003
796.332'092—dc21
[B]   2003047330

This book is available in quantity at special discounts for your group or organization. For further information, contact:
    Triumph Books
    601 South LaSalle Street
    Suite 500
    Chicago, Illinois 60605
    (312) 939-3330
    Fax (312) 663-3557

Printed in U.S.A.
ISBN 1-57243-538-0
Design by Amy Flammang-Carter

CONTENTS

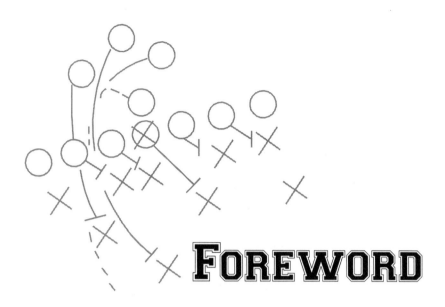

FOREWORD

I have had the privilege of working with many great players during my coaching career in the NFL, some of the best there ever were at their positions. John Mackey was in that elite class, and it was a privilege to coach him and to know him as a man.

John and I broke in to the NFL together in the 1963 season. He was a rookie tight end and I was a rookie head coach for the Baltimore Colts, and I'd like to think we learned from each other during our time together in Baltimore. We listened to what the other had to say—not always an easy task—and that went a long way toward forging a player-coach relationship and a friendship that will last a lifetime.

John revolutionized the tight end position in the NFL. There had never been anyone like him before. He had a combination of power and speed that sometimes made him appear unstoppable when he caught the ball, and he was a devastating power blocker. But many talented people play professional football. It's his work ethic that drives a player to be the best at his position, and John had that sort of determination from the start.

He fit right in on those Baltimore Colts teams that were full of players who had a strong determination to win. He joined Johnny Unitas and Raymond Berry on the field for long after-practice sessions of running precise routes and getting to know each other's tendencies inside and out. It was that extra work that helped turn John into an All-Pro, Hall of Fame tight end.

He was also a superb athlete in a position that rarely saw the level of skill that John brought with him. He expanded the limits of tight ends, averaging 15.8 yards per catch, a figure that most wide receivers would welcome. Those that followed John—players like Kellen Winslow and Ozzie Newsome—owe their success in part to John Mackey's influence on the tight end position. He turned it into a position that defenses had to fear. He could—and did—go deep.

As much as he made an impact on the field, he did the same off the field. He was a leader of men of all color at a time when that was not an easy thing to do, and as the first president of the NFL Players Association he was under tremendous pressure as a pioneer in sports labor. Yet he always maintained his dignity and had the respect of both sides of the issue.

We had something special on the field back in Baltimore, maybe more than we realized at the time. John Mackey was one of the reasons it was special.

—Don Shula

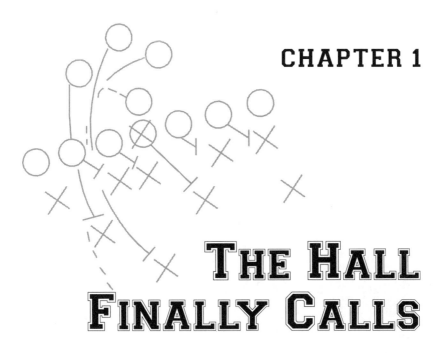

CHAPTER 1

THE HALL FINALLY CALLS

Some people might have believed it would be a cold day in hell before I would become a member of the Pro Football Hall of Fame. That cold day arrived in Minneapolis, Minnesota, shortly before the 1992 Super Bowl between the Washington Redskins and the Buffalo Bills.

I had just returned to my hotel after having lunch with Jack Kemp, Joe Namath, and Roger Staubach. I walked into my room and saw the message light flashing on the telephone. I called the hotel operator and asked for my messages, and the woman on the other end of the phone said excitedly, "Mr. Mackey, you have so many messages, I'll have to send up a computer printout!"

"What's going on?" I asked her, surprised.

"You've just been indicted!" she said.

"Indicted?" I yelled into the phone, and then my wife started yelling in the background, "Indicted? What did you do?"

"Indicted for what?" I asked the operator, and she answered, "You've been indicted into the Hall of Fame."

That's how I found out, in my 15th and final year of eligibility, that I was finally a member of the Pro Football Hall of Fame. I had enemies that may have thought someone should have been indicted for electing me. But most thought it was criminal that it took so long for me to get in.

I was the second tight end in Canton. Mike Ditka was the first, and when Ditka was inducted, he said, "I don't understand how I got in before John Mackey."

Many people didn't. It wasn't because of my performance on the field, that's for sure. In 10 seasons I caught 331 passes for 5,236 yards and 38 touchdowns. My 15.8 yard-per-reception average was unheard of for a tight end. Rick Telander, in *Sports Illustrated*, wrote that I "was the prototype of the modern tight end. Big (6'2", 230 pounds) with the speed of a sprinter, soft hands, and the strength to block defensive tackles and flatten safeties, Mackey turned a bland position into a dangerous, game-breaking one. When Mackey caught a pass in the secondary, defensive backs cringed. Rival players bounced off his oaken thighs like marbles. If somebody didn't hang on, Mackey was gone."

Kellen Winslow, the future Hall of Fame tight end from San Diego, said I was the standard by which tight ends should be measured. "John was really ahead of his time," Winslow said. "His size and speed were unheard of. If I ever came close to playing like John Mackey, it would have been the thrill of my life. I don't think I ever came close to that. To me, the people who belong in the Hall of Fame are people who have had a profound impact on the game. John Mackey should have gone in on the first day he was eligible."

But from 1977 through 1991, I had been passed over. It became embarrassing to the Hall, because each year that passed, more sportswriters wrote articles critical of the process and projected reasons why I was falling short. Most of the articles determined that it was because of my union activity, when I took on the NFL as president of the Players Association and then successfully sued the league for free agency.

But there was another school of thought—one far more personal than conspiratorial—as to why I had been blocked from entering the Hall of Fame for so long. Some people believed it was because of a one-man campaign to keep me out, engineered by a former Colts public relations official who later became a sports columnist at the *Baltimore News American* and, in his final days, the *Baltimore Sun*—John Steadman. Because he was the Baltimore representative in the voting for a long time, it was believed that he was the roadblock to me getting into Canton. There was bad blood between us that went back to the first year I was with the Colts. Buddy Young threw a party to show me what a warm welcome I would get in Baltimore. My agent at the time, Alan Brickman, and my girlfriend, Sylvia, flew in and went to the party. This was a time when players rarely used agents, and I think Steadman got into an argument with Brickman simply for representing me. Steadman shoved Brickman, and we left the party. I don't know if he was the real reason behind all those years I was passed over. It could have been a combination of things, but I never complained about it, because people knew I belonged there. I talked to Steadman about it, and he insisted he was not the reason for me not getting in. I told him that I believed him and that he didn't have that much power. He has passed on now, and whether he held me back or not, I never held it against him.

Here's the way the voting works. There are 38 selectors, primarily members of the media, and they cut down a list of nominees to about a dozen. From there, on Super Bowl Sunday, they meet again to cut the list down to six, in addition to one senior member, and those voted in must get 80 percent of the votes. A player must be retired at least five years to be eligible for induction. It doesn't seem right that players have no say about who gets in the Hall. Brig Owens, a former Redskins defensive back and one of my compatriots with the union, often expressed bewilderment about the process and why I had not gotten in. "If you have a sportswriter who doesn't like you, you're not going to become a member of the Hall of Fame," Owens said. "It took Bobby Mitchell a long time to get into the Hall of Fame because there were a couple of sportswriters who did not like him."

How did I get in finally? I don't know for sure, but the *Washington Post* reported that a Baltimore man, George Young, the former general manager of the New York Giants, worked to break down the wall keeping me out. The *Post* indicated that it was my union activism that kept me out. Ira Miller, a sportswriter for the *San Francisco Chronicle* and the president of the Pro Football Writers Association at the time I was inducted, said he never heard any discussion about problems with my role in the players union in the three years he had been involved in voting deliberations, but he also admitted that I "should have been in sooner."

Whatever the reasons were, I wasn't worried about them or concerned with the past. If there was a problem, it wasn't my problem. When I played, I played to the best of my ability, and it was up to others to make the determination if that was good enough.

I only look ahead, and now I was looking ahead to be inducted into the Pro Football Hall of Fame. It was special to me for a number of different reasons, including the fact that I would be joining some of my teammates from one of the greatest teams that ever played the game, the Baltimore Colts. Jim Parker and Raymond Berry were inducted in 1973. Lenny Moore made it in 1975. Johnny Unitas made the Hall in 1979. And in 1992, I would join them, finally.

The ceremony took place in Canton, Ohio, a blue-collar town about 50 miles south of Cleveland and 100 miles west of Pittsburgh. It is a town befitting the home of a place to honor blue-collar players in a blue-collar sport. This was the home of the American Professional Football Association, founded in 1920, the forerunner of the National Football League. One of the legendary teams in the early days of professional football was the Canton Bulldogs, who won the NFL championship in 1922 and 1923. One of the members of the Bulldogs was the legendary Jim Thorpe (a seven-foot statue of Thorpe greets visitors as they enter the Hall). There were a lot of places with equally significant histories that could have claimed ownership of the Hall of Fame, but it was Canton that started a campaign in 1959 to become the home of the Hall. Two years later it received that designation and got in on the ground floor of something good, probably even better than it could have expected. The city receives national attention every August at the Hall of Fame ceremonies, with thousands of tourists coming to town to watch their favorite players from days past be honored. In addition to that, tourists come to Canton year-round to tour the Hall and see the wonderful exhibits. In its first full year of operation, 1963, the Hall drew 63,000 fans. The number of visitors peaked at 330,000 fans in 1973 and then dropped down to a consistent level of about 200,000-plus. The year before I was inducted, about 209,000 fans passed through the Hall.

I was in good company: it was the year of the maverick at Canton. The 1992 Hall of Fame class included Raiders owner Al Davis and Washington Redskins running back John Riggins. It's well known that Al Davis has made numerous enemies in the league. He came from the American Football League, and, like me, he sued the National Football League. He got a lot more out of it than I did—$18 million. Then there was Riggins, who, while not considered as controversial a figure as Davis or myself, had his share of colorful episodes over his career, including once telling Supreme Court Justice Sandra Day O'Connor to, "Loosen up, Sandy Baby." He once sat out an entire year with the Redskins in a contract dispute, but Riggins also had a great sense of humor. He had NFL commissioner Paul Tagliabue, of all people, introduce him at the Hall of Fame induction ceremonies. When asked why, Riggins said, "Madonna had a headache." Detroit Lions great Lem Barney was also on the inductee list.

Davis had John Madden introduce him. Davis himself had introduced eight Raider Hall of Famers in the past and was clearly looking forward to the moment. At the mayor's breakfast on Friday, he said, "I don't know how I'm ever going to get my speech into the 10 minutes they have allotted me, so I bought some time from Lem Barney and John Mackey. And John Riggins says I can have all of his time."

Fat chance I was going to give up any of my time. It was as sweet a moment for me as for Al Davis or anyone else, though he wasn't kidding about the length of his speech. It ran about 20 minutes, twice as long as the time allotted.

The inductions are a weekend affair, with more than just the induction ceremony. The mayor's breakfast is on Friday morning, followed by a fashion show luncheon at noon and the Enshrines' Civic Banquet on Friday night. Early Saturday morning there is a parade that draws as many as 200,000 people, and then comes the big moment, the induction ceremony.

It was a glorious, sunny Saturday afternoon—there wasn't a cloud in sight—and no one was complaining about being there. Riggins went first, then Davis, and then it was my turn. What a moment! There on the hillside were hundreds of Colts fans, waving their "Colt Corral" banners. There were no fans, perhaps in all of sports, like Baltimore Colts fans, and the continued existence of the Colt Corrals was proof of that. The Colts left Baltimore in 1984, yet these fan clubs stayed in existence all of that time, getting together for special functions and sharing the friendships they had made through football. They wound up embracing the Ravens when that franchise came to Baltimore in 1996, changing their names to Ravens Roosts. But on this day, they were in Canton to share this moment with me, and I couldn't think of better people to share it with.

My presenter was my good friend Jack Kemp, the former quarterback for the Buffalo Bills who became a member of Congress, secretary of housing and urban development, and one of the foremost political leaders in the country. I got to know Jack during the days when I worked with the players union. In 1970, when the NFL and AFL merged, so did the players associations from both leagues. Jack was the head of the AFL players, and we worked together to form the new NFL Players Association. We spent a lot of time together figuring out what we should be doing for the future of the players, and I learned a lot from him. We became close friends; I supported Jack when he first ran for Congress, and I've backed him ever since. The things that he has said throughout his career have been strong and consistent—he doesn't change to suit whomever it pleases. I wanted Jack Kemp to be in Canton with me for this moment. (He might have been there anyway, even if I wasn't being inducted. His son Jeff was the starting quarterback for the Philadelphia Eagles, who were playing that afternoon in the Hall of Fame Game in Canton.) After being introduced, Jack stepped up to the podium to give my introduction:

> I have the honor of introducing the greatest tight end in the history of the NFL, John Mackey, into the Hall of Fame. I was in Philadelphia recently giving a speech and the emcee got carried away and introduced me as the father of the quarterback of the Philadelphia Eagles, and a very distinguished black gentleman stood up in the back

of the room and said, "He doesn't look like Randall Cunningham to me." I am not Randall's daddy. I am Jeff's daddy—although we would like to have Randall's arm and money. But I want to say that my wife and I are thrilled to be among the fans, friends, and family of John Mackey. [It was a rough game for Jack's son, as the Eagles lost 41–14 to the New York Jets.]

Of all his accomplishments—All-American in high school in football, basketball, and track; an All-American in football at Syracuse; named All-Pro three times and to the Pro Bowl five times in 10 years in the NFL; finishing with the Chargers in San Diego after nine years with the Baltimore Colts, I want to introduce John Mackey's greatest accomplishment. Of all the things he has done on this earth, his greatest accomplishment is his dear family: his wife, Sylvia, and his children, Laura, Lisa, Kevin, Sandra, and Butch, and his precious grandchildren, Vanessa and Benjamin. You can't understand John Mackey until you understand his family. You can't understand John Mackey until you know his mother and father. Reverend Walter Mackey is a man of integrity, character, honesty, tenacity, and audacity, and has a great belief in human beings and the Creator. When John was picked by Ben Schwartzwalder to go to Syracuse, coach Schwartzwalder sent him three airline tickets for his mom and dad and for John, but Reverend Mackey said, "We can't accept the airline tickets. We will drive. I don't want you beholden to anybody." John ended up at Syracuse with the great Ernie Davis as a roommate. John was a great player at Syracuse, like Ernie Davis and Jim Brown in the tradition of that school, and he went on to become a great player in the NFL, and today is being enshrined in the Hall of Fame.

I first met John Mackey out on that football field. Unlike Johnny Unitas, I never had the honor of throwing to John Mackey, or playing with him or against him on the football field. I met him in a union meeting. John and I were merging the American and National Football League players unions. When I began that meeting, speaking to all of the player representatives from both leagues, John Mackey didn't say a word. He didn't talk for the longest time. Finally, he just said a very few words, and with those few words he motivated and inspired and moved men from one position to another position, which is the ultimate example of leadership in our society. After the meeting, I asked, "John, why didn't you speak longer?" He said, "Jack, my papa taught me to learn to listen. He said if you listen, you will be the smartest man in the room. You will know what you know, and you will know what other people know as well."

Well, John Mackey was the smartest person in that room.

I believe it was a mistake to call John Mackey a rebel. He wasn't a rebel; he was a catalyst. He was not rebellious; he was a leader. He understood labor and understood capital. He understood the needs of the employees and recognized that you can't have employees without having employers. John was the bridge between black and white in leading the union. Dr. King gave that speech on the steps of the Lincoln Memorial in which he said he dreamed of a day in which America would be free to look at our children not on the basis of the color of their skin, but on the basis of their character and the content of their character. John Mackey is a bridge to that goal. He is making better dreams come true in America, working between black and white, labor and management, between enterprise and working men and women. He cares about this country. He cares about family. He is a man who truly is blessed and recognizes the biblical injunction that those who have been blessed have an obligation to be a blessing to their families and to their communities and to their country and ultimately to the world. I want to give you not only a great football player, not only a great family man, but I want to give you a great American, the great John Mackey of the Baltimore Colts, the next enshrine of the 1992 class.

The hillside erupted with cheers as all those Colts fans got to their feet, and all of a sudden I was back in Memorial Stadium in Baltimore, the place they called the world's largest outdoor insane asylum, running over tacklers after catching a Unitas pass. It was sweet, and I wanted to share that sweetness with everyone there, as well as with the people who were special to me but couldn't be there when I stepped up to the podium to speak:

> Thank you very much, Jack. You know, when I found out I was going into the Hall of Fame, I was with Jack and Joanne and my wife, Sylvia. Jack gave me one of the greatest compliments and I want to share that with you today. When we found out I had been inducted, Jack said, "John, I just want to tell you something. You know, John Unitas never threw you a pass because you were a minority. John threw you a pass because first, he knew you would get open, and second, he knew you would catch it, and third, he knew you would know what to do with it." That made me feel good because it is very important that we evaluate people on the basis of their performance alone. So Jack, you were right. I've got to thank Mike Ditka for getting in the door at the Hall of Fame and making it possible for me to come here. I am going to stand in the door until the rest of the tight ends get in.
>
> You know, it takes a team to get to the Hall of Fame, and I want to introduce you to the team

that was there for me on Mondays after the Sunday games. They were there when it hurt. My quarterback and roommate for 29 years, Sylvia, and my motivating children, because I had to run hard to put milk on the table. Lisa, Laura, would you stand up, and you know I had to run real hard to feed this one, Kevin. [They stood up to the cheers of the crowd, another proud moment for me.]

There are a lot of people I need to thank. I need to start with my father, the Reverend Walter Mackey. He used to say to me when I was in high school, "Son, I know you scored a touchdown, but where are your feet?" I had no idea what he was talking about. I want him to know—he is 87 years old and I know he is watching—I want to tell him first, that I love him and second, that today I know where my feet are. I keep them placed on the ground, so I keep my head out of the clouds. My father also said to me when I was a young boy that if you don't pass in school, you are not going to play on the field. So I always tried to work hard in school. My mother has passed on. We called her Mom Mack. I remember she had a white dress that she used to say she would wear when I was inducted into the Hall of Fame. I know she is watching me today and I want to tell her, "Baby, I love you." I did exactly what she told me the day she signed a note so I could play football in my sophomore year in high school. She signed the note and told me just to be the best football player I could be. Mom, I've always tried to be the best I could be.

I would like to thank Mrs. Church, my English teacher at Hempstead High School, and Mr. Keenen, my math teacher. They guaranteed me that if I carried my books while I carried the ball, they would make sure that I would pass the college boards and go to any college I wanted to, and I want to thank them because they were right. I would like to thank my sister and my brothers because there were six boys and one girl in my family, and they taught me about competition, because I had to fight for my fair share at the dinner table. I would like to thank Jim Brown. He came from Long Island, and I saw him play at Syracuse and in the NFL, and then I believed I could do that same thing. I thank him for that. I've got to thank Ben Schwartzwalder, my head coach at Syracuse, and the rest of the coaching staff there, for giving me No. 88 and not No. 44. No. 44 was a running back. They told me I was a tight end. I thank them for that. I want to thank Syracuse for the great education I got and for preparing me for life after sports. And to the line coach, Joe Szombathy, who is sitting over there. He taught me how to hit, but he taught me something more important. He said, "Son, you will spend four years at Syracuse. I demand that you get more than a touchdown." I got a good education. I thank you, Joe.

And to the Baltimore Colts, I want to say that the first person I met when I joined the Baltimore Colts in 1963 was the equipment manager, Fred Schubach. Freddie said, "I shine your shoes every day. I polish and I clean your helmet. I press your practice uniform. I demand that you play the way you look." I say to Freddie, I am still playing the way you made me look. I would like to thank Don Shula. Don was a rookie coach when I was a rookie, and I will never forget that he said, "The team that is going to win on the field is the team that can make the right adjustment after the ball is snapped." I say to Don Shula, I am still making adjustments after the ball is snapped. And to Jim Mutscheller, who came out of retirement and who was the tight end for the Baltimore Colts years before I came in. He came back to teach me how to play tight end in the NFL. He told me if I never remember anything, remember this, "Just get off on the count," and I am still getting off on the count, Jim. And to Dick Bielski, they thought I would never learn how to run pass patterns, but we spent hours together. They didn't believe we could do it, but we did it, Dick. I had many teammates and I want to thank all of them. It started in Roosevelt, New York, on the playgrounds and went to Hempstead High School and then to Syracuse University and then to the Baltimore Colts. I thank them because I am here because they were there then. They made me what I am. I have always been a team player. I would like to thank the NFL Players Association for electing me president in 1970 and for having enough faith to back me all the way. I love them for that.

You know, it is a little sad because there are no Baltimore Colts today, but it makes me feel good when I look over there and see the Colt Corrals. I see those Colts fans. I want all of you to know that I love you. We never had a losing season, and the fans were our secret weapon.

I thank the NFL Players Association and the Better Boys Foundation for naming the Mackey Award after me. It has been around for 30 years. We raised millions of dollars and helped those who needed help.

You know, ladies and gentlemen, some of my best friends are up there with my mother, and if they had their way they would be here today, like Ralph Jones, the Morgan State athletic director and one of the first guys I met in Baltimore. He actually brought Lisa and Sylvia home from the hospital when I was in training camp. He saw my daughter before I did. He passed on before he had an opportunity to be here and I know he is up there today. And I just wanted to say, Ralph,

I love you. And to Loudie [Loudie Loudenslager, the Colts' biggest and best-known fan]. Loudie, the last time I saw him, he said, "John, whenever you go into the Hall of Fame, I will be there." He was there for every game I ever played with the Colts. I can hear that Colts fight song now, and if someone will throw me the ball, I will run through the crowd. And John Paglio, he was a guy I played with at Syracuse. . . . He called me when he found out I was going into the Hall of Fame. Last month he passed away. I didn't know this, but he had given up open heart surgery to be here, but God took him away. I want you to know, John, that we love you, we love Ann [his wife], and may God bless you.

You know, if I had my way, I would take No. 88 and divide it into two No. 44s, and I would take my roommate [at Syracuse], Ernie Davis, the first black player to win the Heisman Trophy, into the Hall of Fame with me. Thank you. May God bless you. It has been a pleasure.

And that's what it was—a pleasure. It was my time in the sun, and my feet were on the ground, but my head was in the clouds as well. It was that kind of day, to celebrate not just what I had accomplished, but how I did it as well, with the life lessons of honesty and integrity—and color blindness—that I had learned at home from my parents, the lessons I have tried to pass on to young men and women.

One last component of my Hall of Fame ceremony would follow sometime during the regular season that year. One of the traditions is for the player to receive his ring at a halftime ceremony for the team he represented during his career, or, if there were several teams, the one he chooses. That would mean the Indianapolis Colts would have honored me with a halftime ceremony and presented me with my ring, and they desperately wanted to do so. After all, it would be the first such ceremony for a Colts player since the franchise left Baltimore like thieves in the night, unannounced, in 1984.

But I had no intention of letting them do that. I had no connection with the team in Indianapolis, no matter what their record books said. My heart was in Baltimore. The Hall of Fame officials said, "John, you have to go to Indianapolis to accept this ring," and I told them, "I will do it in Baltimore. That's where I played." So I accepted the ring at halftime of an exhibition game between the Miami Dolphins and the New Orleans Saints, played in Baltimore's Memorial Stadium, where I used to catch passes from the great Johnny Unitas. Hosting the game was part of the city's effort to bring an NFL franchise back to Baltimore, which happened four years later when the Browns moved from Cleveland and became the Baltimore Ravens.

There is no other place I would have rather been when the final chapter of my Hall of Fame saga closed. I had come full circle in my professional football career, a ring of honor I was proud of. But the foundation for that career started in the Mackey home.

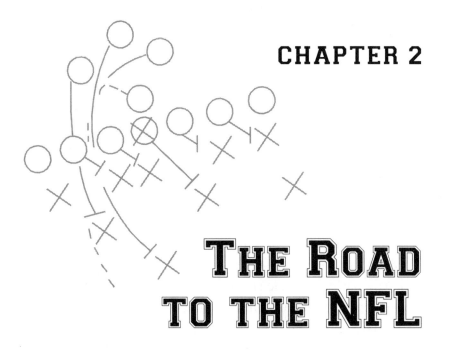

CHAPTER 2

THE ROAD TO THE NFL

I was born on the run and I've been moving ever since. I was born in a taxi on the way to Kings County Hospital in New York on September 24, 1941. We were the kind of kids who came in a hurry. We were always hurrying.

The oldest among the Mackey siblings is my sister, Inez. Then my brother Walter, followed by Larry and Arthur. I'm next and there are two more after me, James and Elijah.

We were a close family, all the siblings, when we were growing up. When my daughter Lisa put her arm through a storm window and severed everything to the bone, all of my brothers were at the house the next day. When something happens within the family, everyone comes. It's not like calling and asking if they're needed; they just come. When I was in college and Sylvia blew the engine of my car, my brothers took the car, told me not to worry about it, fixed the engine, and sent it back up to me.

The patriarch of the Mackey family, and the man who taught us the value of family, was my father, Walter. He was a minister. He and my mother, Dora, met in South Carolina, near Aiken, where they were both born and raised. My father was very light skinned, very fair, and my mother was very dark. This contrast nearly got my family killed, or, at the very least, seriously harmed, in the sort of ugly racial incident that might have poisoned a lesser man than my father.

In Aiken, my father was a successful businessman. He was the general manager of a business called the North American Clay Company—not the kind of position where you would normally find a black man in South Carolina in the thirties. But I think a lot of people believed he was a white man because of his fair skin color—he was part Cherokee Indian with light, straight hair. But things changed one night at a banquet. My father had been named Man of the Year by some kind of organization. Apparently, none of these people had ever met my mother before.

So when my father showed up with my mother, whose appearance left no doubt she was black, all hell broke loose. My father didn't realize what he was in for, but it was clear to him they were no longer welcome in Aiken.

They left town that night, with the owner of the company helping my mother, my sister, and my two older brothers, who were the only children at that time, get out without being hurt or worse. They went to New York, where my father would meet them. He could not accompany them—he was a hunted man.

There were a lot of angry white people in Aiken who felt they had been fooled. Or worse, they saw the truth before their eyes: a black man had the ability to reach a high-ranking level of success right in their backyard, passing by many of them up the ladder. Whatever the reasons, the Ku Klux Klan was chasing my father, so he had to go on the run before joining the rest of the family. He headed west, then north up to Michigan, until he felt certain he was not being followed anymore. Then he headed to New York to join my mother and his children.

This kind of hatred, having their whole lives suddenly uprooted and changed forever because of the fears of a racist community—a community that my father had once been a leader in—should have left Walter Mackey a bitter man. But he was anything but bitter. He became a man of God, a Baptist minister, and never allowed any of us to talk about the color of a person's skin. Even though his church was Baptist, he simply called it a House of God. He believed that if you put a label on something, everyone will start fighting over whose is best. He never wanted anyone judged the way he was judged. He was never accepted because of the color of his skin.

Years later, I got a firsthand look at the deep Southern racism that drove my family away. I went down to visit my grandmother in Aiken when I was about eight or nine years old. I had never been out in the woods to see where my father grew up. My grandmother asked me to go down and get some water from the well, but I had never seen a well before and had no idea what to do. I was in the process of trying to climb down into the well with the bucket to get the water when a white lady came along. "What are you doing, boy?" she asked.

"I'm trying to get some water out of the well, ma'am," I answered.

"Well, you fetch me some water, boy," she said.

The word *boy* had no significance to me. In fact, my father used it often when he was talking to me. I had always been taught to be polite to people and say "Yes, sir" and "Yes, ma'am" when talking to adults. So I answered her politely. "Yes, ma'am, if you show me how to do it, I'll be more than happy to get it." She didn't realize I had never heard the word *fetch* before, so I really didn't know what she wanted me to do.

"How do you fetch it?" I asked.

She thought I was ignorant. "Where you from, boy?" she asked.

"New York," I answered.

"Well, up there they kill blackbirds, and down here they kill black niggers," she said.

I knew what that last word meant, you better believe it.

"Drop that damn pail down the well and then pull it up," she ordered me.

When I pulled it up, I took the water and threw it on her. She started screaming and I stood there, furious, thinking to myself, "Who the hell are you to call me a black nigger?" I ran home and they sent me back up to New York real quick.

When my family first got to New York, we stayed in the city, in the Bronx, with my father's sister. We didn't have a lot of money. We had to leave everything we owned behind in Aiken because we had to leave so quickly. We stayed in the city for some time; I was born there and began growing up there. My two oldest brothers had grown and were in the service. My mother was working and my father spent time building a house on a piece of land in nearby Roosevelt, Long Island. He wanted a better life for us.

A lady from the church named Mother Kitching would take care of my older brother Arthur and me. I thought she didn't really like me, so I didn't want to go to her house. Instead, I would run back home and wait on the stoop. We lived in a big apartment building in the Bronx where you had to have a key to enter, and I didn't have a key. So I would wait, and sometimes I would get into trouble. My father didn't like that; he worried about his children growing up in the city and was trying to find a way to get us out of there.

One time my father sent me to buy something for him at the corner store, and there was a shoot-out in the streets. Somebody was robbing the store, and a person was killed. When I got back home I told my father what happened and why it took so long for me to come home. He thought I was just making it up to explain why I didn't come back right away, but later he found out it was true. I think that pushed him to move us out of the city even quicker than he had planned. We moved out to Long Island and into the house he was building before he had even finished it. We lived in the basement of the house while he kept working on it.

That wasn't all he was working on. My father was determined to build a church there, too. He got all of us and our friends and neighbors to help him build it, hand and foot, all the way. I used to spend a lot of Saturdays helping him.

We made friends with the family that lived behind our house, the Scotts. They had a lot of kids, and my brother Arthur and I used to play all the time with Aaron and Jeff Scott. This is where I think I really learned how to be an athlete. We were constantly playing games together. Everything we did was competitive. "I can beat you here and now, let's race to the corner," was often said. Everything had a competitive angle to it; it's how we played all the time. We didn't have a lot of toys, so we made up games, like stick-jumping. We would cut down a sapling, shave off the bark, and put a point on it. Then we would run, stick it in the ground, and jump up on the side of the garage—almost like pole-vaulting. If you couldn't do it, you weren't one of the boys. So I learned how to stick jump.

One time when I was at Hempstead High, walking by the pole-vault pit, the track coach, Moose Krause, who had gone to Notre Dame, noticed that I was laughing at this kid trying to jump about with a pole. Coach Krause asked me, "Do you think you can do any better?"

I said, "I don't need a stick to jump that."

Coach Krause said, "What do you mean a stick?"

"I can jump that without a stick," I declared.

Then coach Krause explained the intricacies of pole-vaulting to me. "You have to count your steps," he said. "You run down, you hit, you slide the pole in the trough, then you kick, you pull, and you go up."

I tried to do it but I couldn't. I couldn't coordinate sliding and kicking and all of the things you had to do. Turnabout was fair play, so they laughed at me. I went home, but I would be back the next day—with my stick. I held it outside the bus window as I rode to school. After school, I went to track practice and told the coach to move the pole away from the pit and into the grass. Then I used my stick to jump about 11 feet, 9 inches. Coach Krause was freaked out, and that was the day I became a pole-vaulter. I also ran sprints and was on the relay team. Of course I also played football in high school, as well as basketball.

Everything I did as a kid growing up on Long Island prepared me to play professional football. The kids I hung around with played all kinds of games, and most of them involved running. We ran all over the place. If your mother or father said to you, "Go down to the store and buy something," you raced a friend to the store and raced him home. When it was time to go to school, everybody would meet at the corner and race to school. Then we would race home for lunch and race back to school, which was about a mile away. That meant we were racing four or five miles a day. After a while you'd get a reputation as one of the fastest kids in the neighborhood. Then maybe you'd be playing basketball against kids in the next town over, and you'd hear about their fastest kid. Pretty soon you'd have a challenge race around the block.

When I was about eight or nine years old, the first organized sport I played was baseball on a Boy's Club team. I was a left-handed first baseman—I'm a left-hander in a family of righties, except for my father, who is also left-handed. But since everything in our family was a hand-me-down, I had to learn to play with a right-handed mitt. Finally I got a left-handed mitt and was a leftie after that. When I started playing organized sports, it was like I was playing against little kids because I had played against a lot of older guys in my neighborhood.

I was about 5'11", but I could really jump—I was the best leaper on the basketball team. So instead of playing guard, where I should have been, I wound up playing center. I averaged between 16 and 20 points a game, and we won 63 out of

65 games in the three years I played. Our coach was Johnny Mills, and he was a great coach. He really taught us how to play the game, and he knew how to win. Everyone in the school got used to us winning, too. One time when we lost a championship game against Garden City, nobody in Hempstead would talk to us. Hempstead was an area made up of all different kinds of people—white, black, middle class, and poor. Garden City was upper crust. They had no business beating us. We had more talent and we had won every game up until this one. That was what we were thinking going into the game; we decided they didn't even belong on the same court with us. We suffered from a major case of overconfidence, and they had a great system that played off our egos. Garden City played excellent team ball, and we played individual basketball. They beat us by one point, and people wouldn't talk to us for a few days after that. The other students were so upset that the principal had to come on the intercom the next day and remind everyone that it was "just a game." That's not the way everyone in the school felt, though.

I started out playing basketball most of the time, since we also played it outside of school on the playgrounds. As for football, I didn't think I would ever play. I couldn't play as a freshman because my father wouldn't let me. We had a science teacher named Doc White, who was also the freshman football coach. He would go through the classroom and stop at students' desks and ask, "Do you think you're going to pass this course?"

"Yes," we would say, and then he would follow up by asking, "Are you going out for the football team?" If you said no, Doc would reply, "And you still think you're going to pass this course? . . . See you out there!"

Football was very big at Hempstead. Everything was big at Hempstead. We were a powerhouse, and we were strong enough to scrimmage Hofstra University's freshman team. Some guys would fail so they could play an extra year. We were like pros.

But I couldn't go out for the team in my freshman year, and I was on Doc White's list because of it. He figured all the big guys should play football, but I couldn't because my father wouldn't give me permission. Now that seemed strange, since my older brothers had played football, but my father was worried I would get hurt, and he had special plans for me. Maybe it was because I was left-handed like him, but he wanted me to follow him and be a minister, and football didn't fit into those plans.

My father was tough. If you didn't pass in class, you didn't play on the field. That was the rule. No smoking, no drinking, no cursing. You could not be disrespectful. He was the law in my house. He was a very strong and determined man. He decided that he was going to build a church, and he did it. He said, "I'm going to build a community center," and he did it. Whenever there was a problem in the community, when kids were not going to school or were placed in classes that did not stress academics, my father was there. When it came time to vote, the politicians came to my father because they wanted to talk to him about getting the vote in the black community.

My grandfather was named after a slave master, named Walker Mackey. My father was also named Walker, but when he was old enough, he changed it to Walter, because there was no way in the world he was going to be named after a slave master. There is a story in my family about my grandfather that shows how my father developed his pride and determination. My grandfather's white boss would give him torn and tattered clothes for the family, and my grandfather would always thank him. Then he would take the rags and burn them in front of his children—my father. That boss went to his grave believing he was helping the poor black family, that he did something great. My grandfather hated the man for even offering that garbage. He said to his family, "This man believes he has done something great, and does not realize that it's a great insult to me. But I can't tell him that." However, he had to show his family how to respond.

That is the sort of inner strength that formed my father, so when he said I couldn't play football, that appeared to be the end of it. But in my sophomore year, my father was in the hospital having surgery on his vocal cords, which had become cancerous. My mother signed the permission slip for me to play, and that was how we got around my father. She really didn't know much about it, but she said to me, "Just be the best football player you can be." And I was. By the time my father recovered and could talk, the issue was settled. I was pretty good by then and was getting my name in the newspapers.

Football wasn't that big of a deal for me before I started playing—heck, I didn't even know what position I wanted to play when I went out for the team. When Bob Schuessler, our coach, asked me what I wanted to play, a friend told me, "Tell him you want to be an end." So that is how I became a tight end. After that, though, when I saw I was good at it and had some success, it became very important to me, and I wanted to be not just one of the best, but the best there ever was. Just like Jim Brown.

Like every place he played, Jim Brown was a football legend on Long Island. He played at Manhasset High School and won *Newsday*'s Tom Thorp Award as the best football player on Long Island. I saw Jim Brown play when I was in high school, and I would tell everyone that I wanted to be like him. They would laugh at me and say, "You're no Jim Brown. You can't do it." Well, in my senior year I won the same award as Jim Brown—the Tom Thorp Award. But while I wanted to be great, I never thought of myself as being better than anyone else, because my father wouldn't allow it. When I would come home from a game and tell him I scored two touchdowns or something like that, he would ask me, "Where are your feet?" I would say, "Right here," and he would answer back, "Well, keep them on the ground and keep your head out of the clouds."

It was a great time in my life, but one incident was devastating for me. We were playing Uniondale High. I was the punter and went back to punt on a fourth down. I had the option of running the ball, though, so I chose to run. I wound up running over a Uniondale player, a defensive end who had come in to block the punt. I scored, but this kid was out cold and they had to take him off the field on a stretcher. His eyes were rolled up in the back of his head, and they took him to the hospital. I went to visit him there, but this kid's mother attacked me. She was screaming, "You tried to kill my son," and she was choking me. He turned out to be OK, but it was very traumatic for me. I was only 15 years old.

That was one of two times in high school when football didn't bring me joy. The other time we were playing against

Freeport High School, and rain was pouring down on the field. This game was part of a big rivalry for Hempstead. Freeport was the only team to beat us the year before. We were losing this game with a few seconds left when our quarterback, Art Mason, threw me a pop pass across the middle. I caught the ball, broke a tackle, and was running down the sideline for what looked like the touchdown that would have tied the game. An extra point would have won it for us. I was holding the ball so tight that I squeezed it and it popped out of my grasp. The ball flew out of bounds, and the time had already run off the clock, so the game was over. I was devastated! I had let everyone down. I had a touchdown, and we had the game, but I lost it. My mother, bless her heart, sat in the rain for the whole game, but she really didn't know what was going on. She thought we had won, and she came up to me all excited and said, "Great play, John."

A story about my mother: I won a number of awards during my football career, in high school, college, and the pros. I appreciated those awards, but I didn't embrace them or display them, and I lost track of what happened to most of them. After I retired from professional football, my mother found a large box of trophies and plaques in my garage while she was visiting me in California. They were dusty and scuffed up. "John, you should be ashamed of yourself," she said. "These fine awards were earned through a lot of hard work and effort and you should be as proud of them as we are. I'm going to take them home to Georgia [my parents had moved to Augusta] and clean them up and then send them back to you." So my mother carted this box of trophies back to Georgia. About three months later when she called me on this particular day, she said, "I just took my physical and I passed with flying colors. Everything is OK, the blood pressure is great. By the way, John, your trophies are all cleaned up, and anytime you want them, you know where they are." Then she hung up the phone. A half hour later I got a call from my brother Arthur. He told me our mother had just died—her heart had stopped beating. I was in a state of disbelief. It was as if she had been determined to get her life and the lives of her children in order before she passed away. Cleaning up my trophies—the milestones of my football career—was on that list of things to do. Those trophies and awards mean a lot more to me now, and that is why she was so close in my heart on the day I received such a tremendous honor as being inducted into the Pro Football Hall of Fame.

Overall I had a lot of success playing football at Hempstead. I was named a high school All-American, and after I won the Thorp award, coach Schuessler told a reporter, "Johnny's certainly the finest end I've ever coached and maybe the best we've ever had on the island. He can do everything and do it well. He's a rough, tough player on the field and he's going to get bigger. Yet he's the nicest kid you could find."

By now, I saw football as a way to get where I wanted to go. At the time, I wanted to be a lawyer. There were other influences for me in school besides football. Several teachers looked out for me, like my math teacher, Robert Kennan, who took an interest in my education and helped convince me there was more out there than football. Years later I asked him why he had helped me in particular, and he said, "You were different, John. You used to listen to what I said." I had concluded that law was the vocation I wanted to pursue.

But, as I said before, my father had other plans for my future. He wanted me to be a minister. As strong as he was, I wasn't intimidated by him, as some of my brothers might have been. I spent a lot of time with my father, and we were very close. He was probably my greatest hero. He said I could be a minister, a school teacher, or a doctor, but I told him I wanted to be a lawyer. He answered, "I don't pay for lawyers to go to college. There are no jobs for them. When you get through with spending all of this money getting an education, the job won't pay."

I told my father that playing football could earn me a scholarship, and he said, "You play football and get a scholarship, you can go to whatever school you want." But that wasn't the case. My father was very involved in choosing my college. He wanted me to go to the U.S. Naval Academy because I would have been the first black kid to play there. He said to me, "You've got to do it for your race," but I wasn't crazy about that idea. I had never even seen a swimming pool before—I wasn't going to let them drown me.

I wanted to go to Notre Dame at first because we used to hear them on the radio growing up. I was accepted there, even though no one from the school ever even bothered to look at my high school transcript. That wouldn't work for my father. He told me, "You cannot go to Notre Dame. All they did was call on the phone and tell us, 'We've talked to Moose Krause, and if you want to come here, you're in.'"

My father asked them, "Have you gone to the high school and talked to his guidance counselor? Do you know about his grades?"

They answered him, "No, we've talked to Moose Krause and he's in."

My father hung up the phone and said, "You're not going to Notre Dame." His idea was that I would go to college to get an education. If I happened to play football, that was fine, but it was secondary to him.

I was recruited by Indiana, and I visited the campus. That was the first time I had ever been away from home and the first time I had ever taken a plane ride. The coach told me I was accepted, but he also told me that I would have to stay in my place. He actually said to me, "I don't mind, particularly, but you can't date white girls if you come to Indiana."

That was the furthest thing from my mind. I was going to school to play ball and get an education, and he wanted to talk about dating white women? I was just 16 years old at the time.

I was afraid that if I didn't agree to come to Indiana, the coach wouldn't give me a return ticket home.

He said, "Do you still want to come here?" and I told him yes.

"You'll have to sign this paper," he said.

"I can't sign it because my father's not here," I said.

"Take it home with you, have your father sign it, and send it back to me," the coach told me.

When I got on that plane, it was such a relief that they were letting me go home. Indiana never heard from me again.

As much as I wanted to go to Notre Dame, I wanted to go to Syracuse just as much, and there was only one reason for that—Jim Brown. That was where my idol had gone and it was where I wanted to go. And it was fate that I went there, because they did the best job of winning over my parents. When Ben Schwartzwalder met my father, he was the only coach who had done his homework. He knew how to talk to my father. Other coaches phoned and offered my father jobs, but that wasn't what he was looking for. He already had a job; he was a minister. The first thing Syracuse did was send their backfield coach, Bob Bell, who was also one of their best recruiters, to my house. He stayed for dinner, and as soon as he did that, it was all over as far as my mother was concerned. She said, "He's all right, a white man not afraid to eat in a black house." He did it right, saying things like, "What wonderful coffee. Can I have some more? That's the best I ever had." He said all the right things.

Then it came time for us to go to Syracuse to visit the school. I went up once by myself for a visit and came away very impressed. They didn't just show me the gym. I was on my own to look everywhere and talk to anyone I wanted to, such as professors and students. It was a very loose atmosphere, and they didn't put any pressure on me. Then I went for a second visit with my parents. Syracuse had sent us airline tickets to fly up, but my father said, "We'll drive," so we got in the car and drove. They had reservations for us at the Syracuse Hotel, and when we checked in, we had a great big suite. "We can't afford this," my father said, so we checked out and went to a Holiday Inn, even though the school was paying for all of this. My father didn't care. "We don't owe them anything, and we don't want to owe them anything." It took the football staff a day to find us because we didn't leave a message at the Syracuse Hotel about where we had gone. Also, on one of my visits the players who were helping to recruit me told me I could charge all kinds of stuff to the university and take it with me. I did, but my father made me take it all back.

When we finally met with coach Schwartzwalder, he said to me, "Let me talk to your mother and father. You just sit there.

I want to talk to your father first." He told my father, "Reverend Mackey, when we decide to bring a boy to Syracuse University, we look behind him to see what he is made of. I wanted to tell you that this boy here is made of some fine stock." My father sat up. All of the right buttons were being pushed.

So in the fall of 1959, I entered a new phase in my life as a freshman at Syracuse University, and became close to someone who I thought would be my friend for a long, long time. Little did I know that the time I spent with Ernie Davis would be so precious.

CHAPTER 3

SUCCESS AND HEARTBREAK

My time at Syracuse University will always be defined by one of the greatest football players I've ever seen and one of the greatest friends a man could ever have—Ernie Davis. He was my roommate, my teammate, my friend, and my brother. I met Ernie on one of my recruiting trips to Syracuse—he was a freshman there when I was a senior in high school—but I had no idea the impact he would have on my life. Then again, I had no idea what I was in for, period, when I left Long Island in August to go to Syracuse to begin football practice.

My father took me and a friend named Jack Salerno, who was an offensive tackle from Sewanhaka High School, to Syracuse. We became friends during our senior year in high school, when both of us were being recruited. When we got to

Syracuse, I was shocked when we had our first football practice with the freshman squad. I was the only black player on the team! I had never thought about it, and I just assumed there would be more black players. But, then again, I had been warned by Ernie Davis during my recruiting trips the year before. Ernie told me that he was the only black player on his freshman team, a year ahead of me, and that John Brown and Art Baker were the only two the year before. It felt different in that I had always been on teams in high school that had black and white players—certainly more than one black player.

There was another surprise when I got there. I thought I was pretty good because I was an All-American high school football player. But I found out quickly that everyone there was pretty good, and what I had done before didn't mean anything on the field in Syracuse. Walt Sweeney, from Worcester, Massachusetts, was there, as was Dave Meggyesy from Ohio. It seemed like everyone I was going up against or playing with in practice was an All-American.

I lived in Watson Hall, and my roommate, briefly, was Bob Ramsdell, a great defensive end from Freeport High School. I played against him in high school, but he didn't last the year in Syracuse, though I understand he finished school later.

In my sophomore year I met my future wife, Sylvia Ann Cole, from Washington, D.C. She had gone to the McMurry School for Women in Illinois in her first year and then transferred to Syracuse. I was out driving with Art Baker and John Brown, and we offered her a ride. She told us she was a new student. We said, "Come on, we'll take you down to Marshall Street," which was where everyone in school hung out. When we got there John Brown said to us, "Get out of the car." So Art and I got out of the car, and John drove away with Sylvia up to the nearby mountain. About 15 minutes later, Sylvia came running down the mountain. "That damned animal tried to kiss me!" she yelled. I saw her on campus sometimes after that and would say hello to her, but not much more. But then one time I called her because we were going to have a party. I knew she had a lot of good records and wanted to borrow some. She said, "Come on by, and then can you drop me off at the student council office after?" I said sure, so a friend came with me and we picked her up.

While we were driving she said, "Can I ask you a question?"

"Sure, go ahead," I said.

"Why is it that you don't date any of the girls on campus?" she asked me.

That was true—I did prefer to date girls from off campus. There were several reasons we did that. One, they didn't have a curfew like the girls on campus did, and two, we always got a meal at their homes.

I turned to Sylvia and asked, "Do you want a date?"

She said she would love to, so we made a date for that Saturday night, for 7:00 P.M.

Now, I had no intention of going on that date. I was just talking. But Ernie came up to me later and said, "I understand you're taking Sylvia out."

"Sylvia who?" I asked.

"Sylvia Cole," Ernie said.

"No, I was just talking, man," I said. "I never asked her."

"No, man, you're supposed to take her out on Saturday night," Ernie said.

"I got nothing to wear and no money," I said. "I was just talking defense."

"She's a real nice girl," Ernie said. "You really ought to take her out."

"Well, give me some money and I will," I said.

Ernie gave me $5 and lent me his sweater and the keys to his car. I picked up Sylvia and we went to see *Where the Boys Are*, that beach movie with Connie Francis. All of us football players had a card that would get us into the movies for 25 cents. I had that much money myself, so I didn't have to break the five. After the movie, we went out, and it just took off from there. Actually, we became really good friends first, and it evolved into a serious relationship from there, which I give everlasting thanks for. Sylvia has been my guiding light through both good and bad times—my soul and inspiration.

My other serious relationship was football, which did not get off to a good start. The coaches had switched me from tight end to running back in my freshman year, and I got hurt. The offensive guard pulled the wrong way, opened the gates, and I got hit during a scrimmage. I separated my shoulder, but I still played. It was the first time I had ever been really injured. My arm was in a sling and I had to sleep sitting in a chair. If I coughed, I thought I was going to die. I was very apprehensive and started to think I was never going to play again. The coaches had the trainers construct a fiberglass case and rubber "doughnut" to cover my shoulder so that I could play the rest of my freshman year. I played against Army and a few other schools on the schedule, and I thought I did pretty well as a running back. Syracuse did very well that year—the varsity won the national championship. But we had a pretty good freshman team as well, and the varsity had a hard time when they played against us. The captain of our team—the Greens—was Jimmy Wright, and he was a football genius, just brilliant. When we scrimmaged against the varsity, they couldn't run on us. I played one defensive end, Walt Sweeney played the other defensive end, and Dave Meggyesy played behind me at linebacker. Jimmy told us to watch coach Schwartzwalder carefully. Wherever he stopped, that was where the ball was going. "He'll stop there to see how the blocking is at the hole," Jimmy said. Sure enough, they called Ernie Davis to run around right end and we had 11 guys waiting for him. After that, coach Schwartzwalder would use Jimmy like an unofficial coach. During the games, Jimmy would stand next to Schwartzwalder, and Coach, without ever looking over at him, would ask, "What do you think?"

"I think 40-Boom looks good," Jimmy would say, and Coach would send in 40-Boom.

Schwartzwalder was a great coach. His teams won the Lambert Trophy, the honor for the best football team in the East; played in three bowl games, the Orange Bowl in 1952 and 1958 and the Cotton Bowl in 1956; and won the national championship in my freshman year. He was an impressive man. He served with the 82nd Airborne in World War II, won a Silver Star in combat, and was a major by the time he left the service. He turned Syracuse into one of the dominant programs in the country and recruited some great players. The class I came in with was pretty impressive. Sweeney, Meggyesy, and I all went on to have standout professional careers. We won all of our freshman games.

I joined the varsity team in my sophomore year, 1960. As a running back, I was fourth on the depth chart. That meant Ernie, Art Baker, and Allan Weber played before me. Even though I thought I played well at times, I knew I wasn't cut out to be a running back. One of the biggest problems was that I would get hit hard in my thighs, and then they would cramp up. Ernie taught me a trick to help avoid those hits that I later used in my career as a tight end. He said that ball carriers have a tendency to absorb punishment when they are tackled, but if you could hit your man first and use your forearm to keep him away from your legs, then you had a good chance of staying on your feet. I put Ernie's trick to good use and became known as a hard man to bring down.

Going into my junior year, Schwartzwalder said to me, "You can be a second-string running back behind Ernie this year, and then in your senior year we will push you for the Heisman Trophy and All-American. And you can wear No. 44." Now, I desperately wanted to wear No. 44, because that was Jim Brown's number at Syracuse. And that was Ernie's number, too. But then Coach said, "We can also make you the first-string tight end right now." They needed ends more than they need running backs, so that's what I took, because I wanted to play, and I wore No. 88.

Schwartzwalder would tell people that the only player he ever made a mistake on was me. He thought he should have kept me at halfback because he thought I would have been a great running back. One thing's for sure—I probably would have been a better-known player as a running back, because as a tight end they couldn't get me the ball. I was a blocking tight end, and they never really took advantage of my abilities to run the ball in the open field. Once Ernie threw a halfback option pass, a short one for a yard or so to me, and I took it about 50 yards downfield. I held the record for average yards per catch, at about 15 catches for a total of 600 yards. I would catch short passes and run to get the yardage. But it was a college-style running offense, and they didn't get the ball to me very much. Wally Mahle was the quarterback, and he rushed for between 600 and 700 yards that season. So when your quarterback runs for that many yards, and you have a running back like Ernie going for 1,000 yards, you don't use too many passes. In my senior year, I led the team in receptions—just eight for 131 yards and one touchdown catch.

Running back was the glory position at Syracuse under coach Schwartzwalder. There was Jim Brown and Ernie, and later Floyd Little and Larry Csonka—all of them were big stars, and wore No. 44. I still played running back sometimes; in fact, I played five games at running back and five games at tight end in my senior year. Schwartzwalder met with me halfway through the season and said he wanted to get the ball in my hands more, so he would hand it off to me at halfback. Years later Roger Staubach came up to me at a banquet and mentioned one of our games. I had forgotten that we played Navy while Roger was the quarterback there, but he remembered the game well. I ran all over them. I scored two touchdowns and had 63 yards on just six carries. In spite of successes like that, I always felt like a tight end, and that's where I wanted to be, though I still had to learn to play that position the right way.

I was also a great blocker. They never talk about that in the pros because they rate you on how many passes you catch as a tight end—at least they did back then. Sometimes I wiped out the whole side of a line. I realized that on a sweep I could block both the defensive end and the middle linebacker if I got off the ball quickly enough and got the right angles. I was proud of my blocking. End coach Joe Szombathy taught me how to play like that at Syracuse. I used to get so excited that when it came time to play, I'd forget what I was doing or I couldn't see anything. In my frenzy I would hit anything that moved. In my sophomore year coach Szombathy got an idea during spring football to stick me at defensive end. He would say, "Mack, take two steps across and look for the guard pulling. If the halfback is coming to block you on the outside shoulder, he's probably trying to turn you in or set you up for the guard. Chuck him and look to the inside. If he's coming to block you out, to keep you out, jam him down into the pile and watch the guard trying to pull around you, because the play is going outside of you."

Coach Szombathy showed me the movement from the other side of the ball and kept drilling it into me, until eventually it all came together for me. In the seventh game of my junior year season, I caught an 11-yard touchdown pass against Pittsburgh in a 28–9 win, which coach Schwartzwalder called "the greatest team effort since I've been coaching at Syracuse." The week after that, we played the final home game of the season, in Archibald Stadium, against Colgate, and destroyed them 51–8. Then came the biggest game of the season—against Notre Dame, in South Bend. It turned out to be a devastating loss for us, but for me, it was probably the best game of my college career. I saw everything they were doing on defense. It was like slow motion. Actually, the trainers gave me some pills before the game and said they were "calm-down" pills. Of course they were just sugar pills. But I believed the trainer and was able to knock Notre Dame around that day. In the third quarter, on a fourth-and-one, I caught a short pass from quarterback Dave Sarette and went 57 yards for a touchdown. I used a stiff arm on that run that, according to one news account, "almost decapitated George Sefolk, the Irish defender." That's when people started to notice me. There was another article that said, "Maybe Ernie Davis' roommate is the best tight end in the nation."

We lost that game, but it was a wild effort. Walt Sweeney hit one guy who had been holding him, and then Billy Schoonover punched a referee. We were losing 14–0 when I scored, and we were successful on the two-point play to make it a 14–8 game midway through the third quarter. We got the ball on our own 47 shortly after that and scored again, putting us up 15–14. With almost no time on the clock, Notre Dame tried a field goal. They missed, and we headed into the locker room believing we had won the game by one point. But the refs called a roughing the kicker penalty just as the game ended. It couldn't end on a penalty, so they brought us back onto the field, and this time, with the ball 15 yards closer, Irish kicker Joe Perkowski put it through the uprights, and we lost 17–15.

My last big game in my junior year was the Liberty Bowl against Miami. I scored a touchdown in that game, too.

During my senior year, in my last game at Syracuse, we were losing to UCLA and needed a touchdown late in the game to win. I was running back punts at the time, and the Bruins had to punt. The one player we had to watch for on punt returns was Kermit Alexander. He was all over the field. When we were in the huddle, I told everyone, "If someone will block Kermit Alexander, I'll go all the way." Well, Sweeney took Alexander down with a tackle, and when I saw that no one was going to stop me, I went all the way, and we won the game 12–7.

Because I played running back for half the season, I didn't have a statistically big year at tight end, catching just six passes for 65 yards and no touchdown receptions. But I got enough attention throughout my college career that people in football knew who I was. I got to play all of the postseason honors games—the All-American Game, the Hula Bowl, and the East-West Game. I played running back in the All-American Game, played offensive and defensive end in the Hula Bowl, and then just tight end on offense in the East-West Game. I had a big game in the East-West Shrine Game, scoring two touchdowns—a 41-yard pass play and a 69-yarder on a pass from Daryle Lamonica—for the East in a 25–19 win at Kezar Stadium in San Francisco.

One of my most interesting experiences in the East-West Game had to do with a coach from Clemson University. I was the first black player he ever coached. He said to me, "You're the first black I've ever had, and if there are any other Mackey boys up there, I'd like to get some down to Clemson. I'd like to integrate us down there." He had never thought about it until he had a black guy playing for him and doing well. Then it became a question of if you wanted to win, it might mean integrating.

When it came time to play in the College All-Star Game against the world champion Green Bay Packers, the coaches had no clue where to play me. It was just like my senior year, and it was miserable. Otto Graham was our coach, and he didn't particularly like me. The coaches were on me all the time. Dante Lavelli was on the staff, and he would tell me that I would never make it in the NFL. He told the other players to make sure that they didn't throw me the ball if I got in the game. I didn't start—Dave Jencks did. But he got hurt on the first play, so they had to put me in. I played the entire game without getting a pass thrown my way. But my strength was blocking, anyway, and I had a pretty good game, even though the Packers did their best to intimidate me. Ray Nitschke said to me right from the start, "You better not block me. Don't you ever touch me, rookie." But I had no fear of Ray Nitschke, and I took him on.

As disappointing as some aspects of my senior year were, they did not compare to what happened to my former roommate and brother, Ernie Davis.

Ernie Davis was one of the greatest athletes of his time, and a favorite son of Syracuse, as he grew up not far from the school. Ernie was born on December 14, 1939, in New Salem, Pennsylvania. His parents separated shortly after his birth, and his father died a little later in an accident. He spent his early years in Uniontown, near Pittsburgh, in coal-mining country, raised by his grandparents. At the age of 12, Ernie moved to Elmira, New York, to live with his mother and stepfather. He went on to be a star athlete at Elmira Free Academy school. He was a high school All-American in football and basketball (he led his basketball team to 52 straight wins) and also played baseball, winning 11 high school letters. He had all sorts of college offers, from UCLA to Notre Dame, but he decided to go to Syracuse, 90 miles from Elmira. Like me, he was drawn there in part because of the presence of Jim Brown, who helped Syracuse recruit him. It also didn't hurt that coach Schwartzwalder made 30 recruiting trips to Elmira.

Ernie was a hard runner. At 6'1", 205 pounds, he ran through the freshman opposition (he played defensive back as well as halfback). His freshman team was undefeated. When Ernie helped lead Syracuse to the national championship in his sophomore year, he was named Most Valuable Player of the Cotton Bowl, as Syracuse beat the University of Texas 23–14. Ernie had a pulled hamstring but still scored two touchdowns, in spite of what turned out to be an ugly scene. Someone from Texas directed a racial slur toward John Brown, which started a bench-clearing brawl just before halftime. That night Ernie was supposed to receive his MVP award at a banquet, but bowl officials refused to invite black players, so the entire Syracuse team refused to attend.

Ernie continued to be a star as a junior with an All-American season, running for 877 yards and a school-record 7.8 yards per carry. He finished his senior year with an equally impressive 823 yards and a 5.5 yard-per-carry average. His total 2,386 yards rushing and 220 points scored broke both of the records held by the great Jim Brown. He had a life that seemed destined for something great.

Ernie and I used to talk about our big plans for the future during long nights at the Stadler "Hilton," the athletic dormitory behind Archibald Field.

"Man, I'm gonna be the best," Ernie said, in that rich, laughing tone of his. "Ernie Davis, professional football player. It has a nice kind of ring to it, right, roomie?"

We lay in our bunks in the dark, talking about our dreams. This was the age of Camelot. John Kennedy was in the White House, and all of America was dreaming of a bright future. It was a new frontier, and Ernie and I were going to be part of it. There we lay, two of only four black players at Syracuse, planning endless possibilities.

"The NFL is where it's at," Ernie said. "Jim Brown has it all, man! I'm gonna be another Jim Brown."

"You still wanna be a lawyer?" Ernie asked me.

"Yeah, man," I said, laughing.

"You're crazy," Ernie said. "You're good enough to play in the NFL when you graduate. The money's great. You can be a lawyer any time after that. Of course, I understand your doubts. You're not as good as me."

"Not as good as you?" I answered incredulously. "Not as good as you? What's your number, man?"

"Forty-four," Ernie said.

"What's mine?" I asked.

"Eighty-eight," he said.

"Well, then somebody at this school knew that I was twice as good as you," I said. "That's why they gave me 88." That was our running joke.

Sometimes when I was with Ernie in his senior year, he would get nosebleeds for no reason. I didn't think much of it at the time, and I certainly didn't realize it was a sign that something was wrong. What could be wrong? Ernie won the Heisman Trophy and was named the top college football player in the country. He was the first black player to win that honor. He was poised to start what should have been a brilliant NFL career, having been drafted by the Washington Redskins in 1961 and then traded to the Cleveland Browns for Bobby Mitchell. He had a chance to have it all, and he deserved it.

During the postseason honors games that followed Ernie's senior year, I started to get worried about him. The All-American Game was in Buffalo that summer; Ernie didn't look like himself on the field. He was going down after just one hit, and he seemed to have lost his speed. The coaches stopped giving him the ball. I first thought Ohio State coach Woody Hayes was trying to showcase his own player, Bob Ferguson, who Ernie had narrowly beaten for the Heisman (it was the second closest voting in the history of the trophy). I kept wondering, "Why don't they give the ball to Ernie? They're trying to show him up."

But that was not the case. Things got worse quickly. In training camp for the College All-Star Game, Ernie complained of fatigue. He left camp to have some tests done, and the rumors started about how sick Ernie really was. We talked on the telephone, and he said to me, "Nothing to worry about, roomie. This is just a temporary setback. No problem."

But there was a big problem, and the news came out shortly after our conversation. Ernie Davis had leukemia. Back then there was no talk of remission—it was a death sentence.

Ernie refused to act like a man who was dying, though. He reported to Browns training camp, which caused a furor because Cleveland coach and general manager Paul Brown didn't want to dress Ernie. Brown was a no-nonsense guy, and he didn't want a sick running back in uniform for their first exhibition game in August of 1962. But owner Art Modell insisted that Ernie be allowed to dress. He wanted Ernie to be able to say that he had played in at least one NFL game. But the issue became moot when Ernie was hospitalized while he was in Cleveland. The stories in the newspaper said Ernie was going to die. I called him up and told him I was coming to see him, and Ernie did everything he could to put up a brave front on the phone. "It's no problem, roomie, everything's fine." I thought to myself that if everything was fine, then Ernie Davis would be in an NFL uniform. Buddy West, who ran track at Syracuse, and Bobby Houston, a high school friend, drove down from Long Island to Cleveland with me to see Ernie in the hospital. After seeing him, I thought maybe Ernie was right. Everything *was* fine. He looked robust sitting in bed, a great physical specimen. "No way he is going to die," I assured myself.

Ernie was released from the hospital shortly after our visit, and I stayed in Cleveland to hang out with him. He was introduced before the start of an exhibition game, and the crowd gave him a long standing ovation. It unnerved me, because it was the kind of ovation a person gets when the crowd knows they are not going to see him again. Then, when a bunch of us were going to an indoor track meet, some stout, bearded, middle-aged man stopped Ernie in the street.

"You Ernie Davis?" the man asked.

"No, sorry," said Ernie, who was shy.

"Good thing, because if you were Ernie Davis, you're gonna die," the man blurted out.

I went after the guy. I wanted to kill him, but Ernie grabbed me and held me back. "Ignore it, roomie," he said. "There's nothing to it."

But there was something to it, although neither of us wanted to talk about it. Ernie was already finished for the 1962 season, but he talked about coming back to play in 1963. He even wrote about his experience for *The Saturday Evening Post.* "I was never in pain, and I never felt sick," he wrote. "That was the hard part."

Now by this time, starting my senior year, I had changed my mind and decided to go into the NFL after I graduated from Syracuse. So the way things were going to turn out, Ernie and I would be rookies in the same season and would compete for Rookie of the Year honors.

"Finally we're going to know who is better," Ernie said.

"Yeah, everyone in pro football is going to decide it finally," I answered.

"As far as I'm concerned, the competition is good, but we know that I'm better," Ernie said.

"You're better?" I said, in a mocking, incredulous tone. "You're better? What's your number, man?"

"Forty-four," he said.

"What's mine?" I shot back, like we had done so many times before.

"Eighty-eight," Ernie said.

"Somebody has known all along that I'm twice as good as you," I said, and we laughed for the last time. A few months later, Ernie Davis died.

The whole football world mourned. Jim Brown spoke for many when he said, "The way he carried himself, the way he did not drown in his own tears, the way that he did not hang on his sickness, the way that he functioned as a human being under all those conditions was tremendous courage." That's what Ernie Davis' gift to all of us was—his courage.

The next summer, I would prepare for my new career in the NFL, a career that Ernie Davis convinced me I was made for, a career that I would not be able to share with the man who was one of the greatest football players I've ever seen, a man who was my brother. Before I attended the official signing ceremony staged by the Baltimore Colts, the NFL team that drafted me, John Brown and I were asked by Ernie's mother to go with her to Cleveland to pick up Ernie's personal effects. We drove from Syracuse to Cleveland to do that, and then drove back the next day. I took exams the following day, then flew to Baltimore for the press conference.

But there was one piece of business that I had to finish up before I became a professional football player. When I first got to Syracuse, a man gave me $300 a month. I never asked for it. It just came, and I accepted it. When I was finished with school and about to sign my first professional contract, my father had to co-sign with me because I was under 21. Before he signed, my father asked me if anyone ever gave me anything. I told him about the $300 a month, and my father said, "I won't sign unless you give him his money back."

I thought my father was crazy. But he insisted. "You take that money back and you tell that man that you appreciate the fact that he gave it to you when you needed it, and now you're giving it back so he can give it to the next kid. Do that, or else I don't sign the contract and you don't play professional football."

While my father waited outside the office, I met with my benefactor and told him I was paying him back. Then I gave him a check. He couldn't believe it.

I know now that it was the right thing to do, but at that moment I hated my father. Everyone else was taking money. Why did I have to give mine back? That's what I thought, but I never said it, because you never talked back to my father. He wanted me to be a lawyer or minister or something other than a football player, but he didn't get that wish. (It turned out that one of my father's sons did become a minister—my brother Arthur, who is a pastor out on Long Island.) I graduated with a degree in economics from Syracuse, but I was going to play football. However, if I was going to make a living as a football player, my father would make sure I would be an honest one. That would not be easy in the NFL.

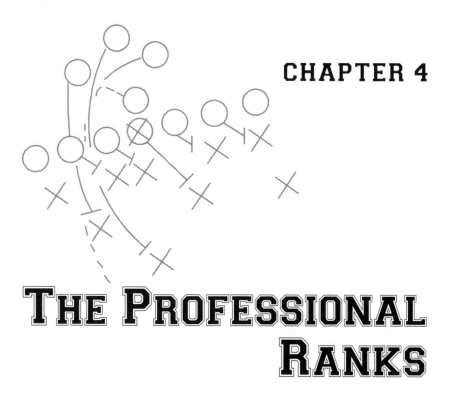

THE PROFESSIONAL RANKS

When I was ready to find a team, I desperately wanted to be drafted by the New York Giants. I grew up on Long Island watching the Giants play on television, and, like every kid, my dream was to play for the hometown team. So I was crushed when they passed me over, and I carried the grudge onto the football field. The first game I played in the NFL was against the Giants, and the first NFL pass I caught was for a 70-yard touchdown. I ran all the way over to the Giants sideline and screamed at their head coach, Allie Sherman, "You should have drafted me." Every time I saw Allie after that we joked about it, and he would say, "I should have drafted you."

But the Giants weren't the only professional football team in New York. These were the strangest times a college kid could have found himself in. We were the ammunition in the war between the National Football League and the upstart American Football League. In New York the AFL team, the New York Titans (as they were called then), got off to a rough start when the league began in 1960. But now they were owned by a high-profile, wealthy man named Sonny Werblin, and he was determined to make the Titans the number one football team in New York.

Werblin was friends with the chancellor at Syracuse University. He came to Syracuse and had the chancellor send for me. I had never had the chancellor send for me, and I thought I was in trouble. When I got into the office the chancellor introduced me to Werblin. "He's got something he wants to talk to you about," the chancellor said. "Go have lunch with him."

As we were walking out the door, the chancellor yelled to me, "John, don't believe a word he says."

We drove to lunch in Werblin's limo, and he told me that he had just bought the Titans and he was changing the name to the Jets. There was a new stadium being built for the New York Mets in Queens between the two airports, and the Jets would play there as well. He pointed out that I grew up about 15 minutes from where they would be playing, and he wanted me to play for them. He said he would offer me triple, even five times whatever the NFL was going to pay me. "I have to sign a player who was raised eight miles from where we play on Sundays," Werblin said.

At the time, though, my dream was to play in the NFL. In fact, I had already signed a contract with the Colts, but no one knew about it. I signed a contract during my senior year at Syracuse, but I wanted to play lacrosse first. So they put the contract in a vault, and no one could do anything with it or say anything about it until I finished lacrosse season. On May 28 the Baltimore Colts, in a press release under the heading of Baltimore Colts News, announced that they had "signed Syracuse's John Mackey." The *Baltimore Sun* had a similar headline, with a picture of me signing this purported contract with my agent, Alan Brickman, Colts coach Don Shula and general manager Don Kellett standing in the background—all a staged show.

"John Mackey of Syracuse got the red-carpet treatment and all the 'hoorah' that goes with it yesterday as the Colts announced his signing during a special press conference at the Sheraton-Belvedere Hotel. The Colts number two draft choice last winter appeared unimpressed by all the hullabaloo of klieg lights and popping questions as he sat flanked by his attorney, Alan Brickman, and Colts coach Don Shula to his right and Colts general manager Don Kellett to his left. . . . Mackey's signing was delayed due to his participation in spring sports, notably lacrosse." I had just come from helping Ernie Davis' mother collect his belongings in Cleveland after he passed away and was not in the best of spirits for this event. It showed, and many of the questions from reporters dealt with Ernie and my relationship with him.

With the Baltimore Colts, I saw a chance to play for a team that already had a championship tradition, a team with such great stars as Lenny Moore and Raymond Berry, as well as a quarterback that any receiver would feel fortunate to play with, the great Johnny Unitas. The NFL was where my future was.

The Colts were born in the All-America Football Conference in 1946, when the bankrupt Miami Seahawks were purchased and relocated to Baltimore. After a contest, they were renamed the Colts and began play in 1947. They were not a very good team in those early days, but they still managed to enter the NFL when the AAFC and the NFL merged in 1950. But it was a short-lived NFL franchise, folding after one season because of financial problems. There was no professional football in Baltimore for two years, until the commissioner at the time, Bert Bell, said that if the city sold 15,000 season tickets within six weeks, the NFL would put a franchise in Baltimore. In the fifth week the city reached the goal, and in January 1953 the NFL's Dallas franchise moved to Baltimore and was renamed the Colts. What's interesting is that the team kept the colors—blue and white—from when they were in Dallas.

The man who owned the new Baltimore team was the same one who owned the team when I arrived—Carroll Rosenbloom. He hired Weeb Ewbank as head coach in 1954, and they built a championship team and created a winning tradition in Baltimore. More than that, they helped set up one of the greatest moments in the history of the league. The Colts won the NFL championship in 1958 by defeating the New York Giants, in sudden death overtime, 23–17, at Yankee Stadium in New York. Fullback Alan Ameche burst over the goal line for the win in what has been called the greatest game in the history of the NFL, the game that many credit for putting the NFL into the national spotlight. They won the league championship again in 1959, defeating the Giants 31–16 in Baltimore.

The man who led the Colts to this winning tradition on the field was the greatest quarterback to ever play the game,

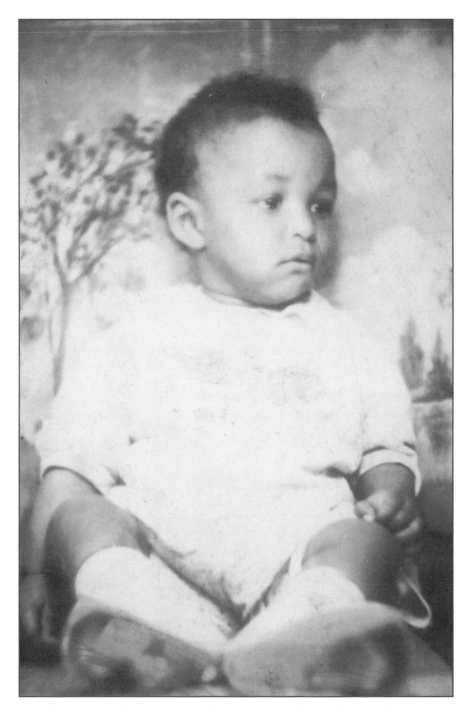

I was born September 24, 1941. *Photo courtesy of the Mackey family.*

I married Sylvia on December 28, 1963. Also pictured are my parents, Walter and Dora (on the right), and Sylvia's parents, Laura and Joseph Cole. *Photo courtesy of the Mackey family.*

I signed a contract with the Colts after being selected as their number one draft choice in 1963. My attorney, Alan Brickman, sat beside me, and coach Don Shula (left) and general manager Don Kellett stood behind me and watched. *Photo courtesy of AP/Wide World Photos.*

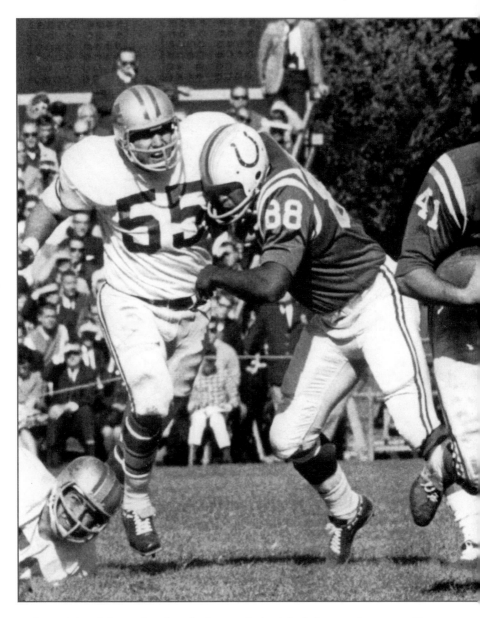

Before I joined the Colts, they had struggled with their running game. But that changed when they saw my explosion off the ball. Tackle Jim Parker and I helped pave the way for backs like Tom Matte, shown here running past Alex Karras and the Detroit Lions. *Photo courtesy of* The Detroit News.

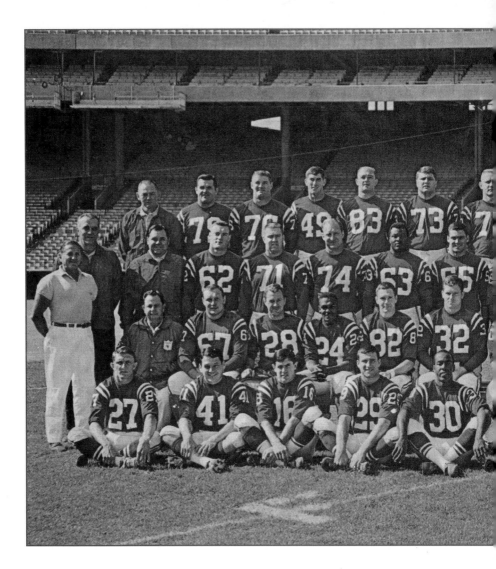

The 1967 Baltimore Colts were a tremendous squad, one of the best I ever played on. We went 11–1–2, scored 394 points on offense, and allowed only 198 points on defense. But those were the days before the expanded playoffs; we didn't even end up playing in the postseason. I caught 55 passes for 686 yards and three touchdowns that season, and I went to the Pro Bowl. *Photo courtesy of the Mackey family.*

Here I am along with Colts teammates Lenny Moore (left) and Johnny Unitas (center) signing a football with the signatures of all of the 1967 Pro Bowl players on it. *Photo courtesy of the Mackey family.*

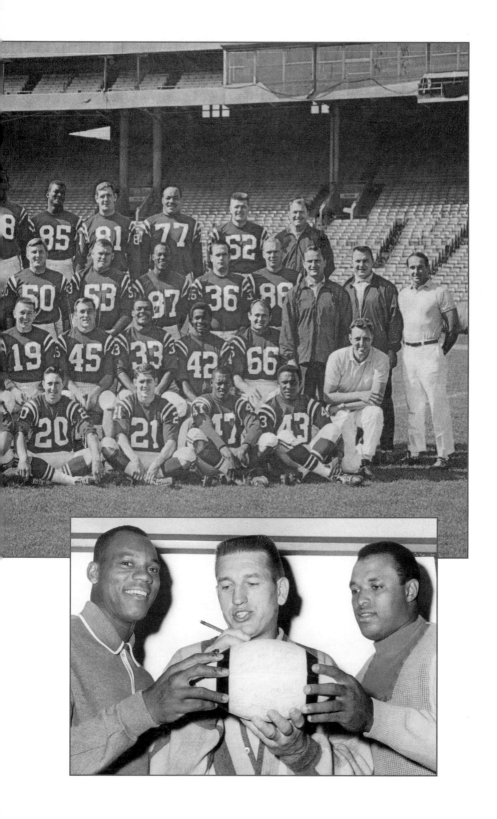

Like any good man, I was only as good as my family. Fortunately I have a great family, thanks to the efforts of my lovely wife, Sylvia, the guiding force in the Mackey clan. She raised three wonderful children: Lisa and Kevin (shown here) and our youngest, Laura (who was not yet born when this picture was taken). All three went on to graduate from college and build their own lives. Of all the things I have done, there is nothing more important to me than the legacy of my family. *Photo courtesy of the Baltimore Sun.*

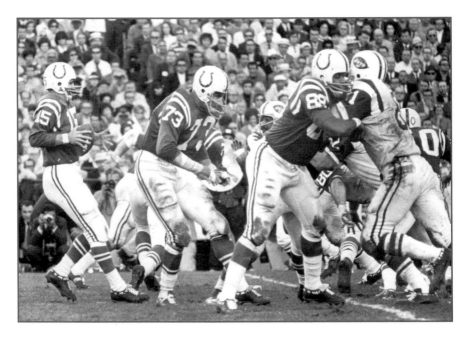

When Johnny Unitas went down early in the 1968 preseason, Earl Morrall (holding the ball) stepped in and led us to a 13–1 record and the Super Bowl. But he couldn't match the New York Jets. He threw three interceptions in the most devastating loss of my career, a 16–7 defeat in Super Bowl III. *Photo courtesy of Vernon J. Biever.*

Johnny Unitas. The story of Johnny U has been well documented. He came out of the University of Louisville, but failed to make the Pittsburgh Steelers. After he was cut, Unitas wound up playing semipro football for a year, hardly the place you would expect to find a future NFL star quarterback. And when he was signed by the Colts in 1956, he was a backup for George Shaw. When Shaw got hurt, Unitas took over and began rewriting the NFL record books. He threw 24 touchdown passes in 1957, 19 in 1958, 32 in 1959, and 25 in 1960. He threw touchdown passes in 47 consecutive games from 1956 to 1960. This was the man I would be catching passes from. Being in a huddle with Unitas was like being with God. It was the chance of a lifetime, and one I will always treasure. I had my first beer ever with John. He invited me to have one after practice once, and even though I had never had a beer before, I had not one, but two with Unitas. I couldn't say no to someone whom I hero-worshiped. It was devastating when John passed away in 2002 from a heart attack.

Even though I wanted a chance to play for the Colts, I had reservations—deep reservations—about moving to Baltimore. I even told Rosenbloom that I wouldn't play for him. I had been in that city before. When I was a kid and my family would go back to South Carolina to visit my grandmother, we used to drive on Route 40, which runs right through Baltimore. We purposely never stopped there, because it was definitely a Southern town and was definitely segregated. Once when I was eight years old, we were passing through Baltimore and we needed to use the bathroom. There was an Esso station my father knew of that allowed blacks to use their bathroom. We stopped, and he went into the bathroom. I wandered across the street to a hamburger joint. I wanted a hamburger bad, so I ordered one. The man said he would sell it to me, but I had to go to the back to pick it up. I figured that was fine with me—I was eight years old, from Long Island, and didn't know any better. I didn't know this was a big deal. Now, I had to go to the bathroom, too, so I used theirs. When I came out, a guy started screaming at me, "What the hell are you doing in there, can't you read?" There were two bathrooms, one for blacks and the other for whites. He yelled at me, "Why did you go in there?" I said, "Because it was the clean one." My father saw what was happening, came over and got me, and apologized. He threw me in the car and we took off. I never got my hamburger or my money back, and I wondered why the hell my father had apologized. It was never explained to me, but I never forgot it, and I told Rosenbloom that I wasn't playing in Baltimore until I got either my hamburger or my money.

He sent his private plane to pick me up. Alan Brickman, Sylvia, and I flew in on the plane to attend a party in Baltimore thrown by Claude "Buddy" Young, a former Colts running back who was now working for the team in the front office. He was one of the first black players in professional football, and he had a remarkable career for a guy who was just 5'4" and weighed only 175 pounds. Over nine years, Buddy carried the ball 597 times for 2,727 yards, a 4.6 yard-per-carry average; caught 179 passes for 2,711 yards, a 15.1 yard-per-catch average; and had 21 touchdowns. Now he was the organization's designated black official for dealing with the black players. He told me, "I just want you to know that I sign all of the black players," and he expected to sign me. I told him to deal with my agent, but no one in the league liked to work with agents back then. It was unheard of, but it was the way I wanted to do business, a professional way. Buddy came up to Long Island to meet my parents, and he laid some cash right on the table to show how much he was going to offer me. He kept putting $100 bills on the table, at one point putting 10 of them in front of my father and more in front of my mother. My father sat there and let Buddy put all of that money in front of them. Then my father picked up my mother's pile, picked up the pile in front of himself, and put the entire pile of $100 bills in front of me. He turned to Buddy and asked, "Are you giving this money to us?" Buddy didn't know whether to say yes or no. "Because if you're giving this to us, we're going to take it. But if you expect John to sign, he already told you to talk to his lawyer. If it's a gift, thank you. We'll take the money. But you still haven't signed him." Buddy took the money back and dealt with my agent. But I sat there thinking to myself, "Why don't we just take the damn money?"

The Colts didn't want to deal with an agent, but they didn't know that he stood up for them. Despite my desire to play in the NFL, Werblin was putting the full-court press on me to play for the Jets. The Colts were doing everything they could to keep me away from contact with the Jets. In fact, Buddy Young came to Syracuse and stayed there, actually baby-sitting me for a while. I found out later that he was also monitoring my phone calls. Brickman advised me, "The only thing you have is your word." So I kept my word and lived up to it. When I became president of the union, if somebody gave me their word but then reneged on it, it was devastating because I had this thing about principles and my word. I've always felt that if I had been faced with this decision any earlier in life, I would have probably played for the Jets and taken the money. I would have had no loyalty. But then I guess I'm better off because I'm not that kind of person.

It was difficult to figure out what everyone's angle was. I soon learned that they played by different rules in the business of the NFL than I was brought up with. I visited the Colts once, before I signed, and Rosenbloom took me around the locker room. He introduced me to Unitas, who looked at me and said, "Keep your eye on him [Rosenbloom] because he'll fuck you." Rosenbloom replied, "That's our John," as if it were a joke. But it was no joke.

They were clearly not thrilled that I brought Brickman with me. He and his wife were put up by the Colts in a small hotel room—a closet, really—with no windows, while I had a big suite, and Sylvia had a big room full of flowers right off of mine.

When I got to training camp, one of the first things that hit me was that while it wasn't totally segregated, black players had a tendency to sit in one area and whites in another. I don't think it was because of some sort of unwritten rule but instead because each group felt more comfortable and they talked about the things they enjoyed. On the other hand, it was totally integrated where the rookies sat because we were all in the same boat. It didn't matter if you were a Southerner or whatever, you were just trying to make the team. I noticed that after I had been in Baltimore for a while, this pattern started to break down, but there were always some guys who would feel more comfortable being around their roommate or closest friend, whomever that was. The roommate situation was originally set up in such a fashion that if the team had an extra white or an extra black player, that guy always had his own room. I looked at it as an advantage—I always wanted to have my own room. That system changed only after Vince Lombardi decided that the Green Bay Packers would room together alphabetically. Then everybody did it that way.

The rookies stuck together because we were not black or white. We were green, as in unseasoned and uneducated in the ways of the NFL, and that meant taking your share of rookie harassment. One time I was getting undressed in front of my locker after practice. Gino Marchetti had a dead rabbit tied to a string hung from the ceiling, but I didn't notice it. When he let the string down, this dead rabbit was right in my face. I yelled and ran out of the locker room.

The first time I joined a huddle at practice, John Unitas, Lenny Moore, Raymond Berry, and all those other great players were standing around me. I couldn't even speak. I was like a kid. I couldn't believe I was there. I wouldn't say anything in the huddle because I was in awe. And, at first, I had a hard time hearing Unitas in the huddle. I wanted to call him "Mr. Unitas." I didn't know if I should talk to him, so I would talk to Raymond Berry instead, and he would talk to Unitas. He would tell Unitas, "Mackey can get open." Then after a while we developed a relationship, and I got to know people, and then I felt it was all right to speak up and say something. Unitas would ask, "What have you got?" and I would say, "I can beat him deep."

One time during a practice in my rookie year, Unitas called a play, and I released to my side. One of our linebackers, Bill Pellington, clotheslined me and nearly knocked my head off. I was messed up. I lay on the ground and had to be helped up and to the sidelines. They had to give me some smelling salts before I could go back out. When I got back into the huddle, I was too mad to be intimidated by Unitas or anybody else. I wanted to get back at Pellington. I started yelling in the huddle, "Throw it to me, throw it to me." Unitas said, "Shut up, I'm the only one who talks in the huddle." He called a few plays, and we ran them. Then he touched me on the leg in the huddle and said, "Are you ready to get him now?"

"I'm ready," I said.

"You're acting too anxious, he knows you're coming," said Unitas.

He called a few more plays and then called a 34 trap, where I had to take on the middle linebacker—Pellington. I struck him harder than he had ever been hit. I knocked him down, tore off my helmet, and stood over him, yelling. Pellington looked up at me and said, "Rookie, welcome to the National Football League, but when the fighting starts, keep that helmet on."

I wasn't the only rookie, of course. One rookie had everyone watching—the Colts' new head coach, 33-year-old Don Shula, one of the youngest coaches in the history of the NFL. Ewbank had coached the Colts during their championship run, but after three seasons of mediocre records—a 21–19 mark—he was fired, and Rosenbloom hired Shula, who had played corner-back for Baltimore from 1953 to 1956. (Ewbank would get his revenge in Super Bowl III.) After retiring as a player in 1958, Shula went into coaching and was a defensive coordinator when he was asked to come to Baltimore. He would go on to become one of the all-time great coaches, leading the Colts to seven straight winning records (73–26–4) and the 1968 NFL championship and Super Bowl. But he would really make his mark with the Miami Dolphins, coaching there from 1970 to

1995, earning two Super Bowl championships and leading the Dolphins to a perfect 17–0 record in 1972. When he retired, Shula had an overall coaching record of 347–173–4.

When I got to camp, Shula told me I was sixth on the depth chart for tight ends (actually, just like at Syracuse, Baltimore debated trying me at running back). There were five ahead of me, he said.

"When do you expect me to be a starter?" I asked.

"When you can beat out the other five guys," Shula said. "You're behind."

"What can I do to catch up?" I asked.

"I'll bring in Jim Mutscheller to teach you the system," he said. "Jim has been one of our great tight ends from the past. If you don't mind sleeping in the afternoon, you can practice in the morning, and Jim can tutor you in the afternoon before the late practice."

So that's what I did, along with three-a-day practices. Jim taught me the key to playing tight end, something I would teach to anybody who wanted to learn—make sure to get off on the start. That becomes important in terms of getting out on the pass pattern and especially in blocking a 300-pounder when you're only 217 pounds. Anytime you hit an object that is standing still, you can move it. That is one of the keys to being able to really come off the ball and block.

The whole rookie season was one big learning experience. One time we were in a game and the two-minute warning was coming up. The clock was just about to stop, but Unitas called a timeout before it could. Everyone wanted to know why he was calling a timeout, and it was because he wanted to call a play before Shula sent one in. He called right flank left, dipsie doodle on two. I was wondering to myself, "What the hell is a dipsie doodle?"

"What should I do?" I asked.

"Stay out of the way," Unitas growled.

That meant stay and block, so I stayed in. Raymond Berry ran downfield, grabbed his ankle, rolled over, jumped up, and caught a pass for a touchdown. That was a dipsie doodle.

Playing with Unitas as a rookie was like going to the highest football university in the land. John would tell me to go down and hook across the middle. I would go down and hook across the middle a hundred times. One day Unitas came to me and said, "The object of the game is to get open. So don't hook across the middle if it ain't open. I can see." That's when I learned to go down, hook, and slide to the outside if it's covered, and let Unitas make the adjustment. When I first started out, I wanted to do exactly what he said because I was afraid to make a mistake. But after a while, he showed me that the object of the exercise was to get open.

I also learned a lot from Raymond Berry. He showed me the value of knowing if the man who was covering me was right-handed or left-handed. He said if the guy is right-handed, you make him do everything on his left foot, and if he is left-handed, make him do everything on his right foot. He showed me how to count steps to make a guy go off on the foot you wanted him to. I learned from Raymond that you could find out your opponent's strengths and weaknesses by watching films. He told me, "No matter what someone says to you, don't let them get you out of your game." I had that happen to me early in my career. A guy yelled, "Watch out," and I missed the ball.

Some things, though, I didn't want to learn. Willie Richardson was my roommate when we were rookies, and we used to eat breakfast together at the Double T Diner. Jim Parker, the great offensive tackle, looked out for the black rookies, and he asked me once how I was doing, where was I staying, and all that. He asked where I was eating. "Every morning at the Double T Diner," I said. He laughed, but didn't say anything. He kept asking me where I ate breakfast, and I would tell him. "Why are you always asking?" I wanted to know.

"I think I'd like to come with you tomorrow and have breakfast," Parker said.

The next day we met and had breakfast at the Double T, and Parker couldn't believe it. The Double T Diner was segregated, and blacks were not supposed to eat there. I just went in there and ate. I didn't know. Jimmy freaked out.

Back then, if you were a black rookie or a new black player, you were turned over to somebody like Jim Parker or Lenny Moore. They were supposed to show you where to find a place to live and all of those kinds of things. At that point in Baltimore, blacks didn't live on one side of town; they lived in the inner city. Jewish people lived on the west side, in the Pikesville area, and the Wasps lived over in the Towson area. There was also Polish Town and Little Italy and all kinds of ethnic neighborhoods.

Willie and I stayed at a place called the Boxwood Lodge. We had been told that they had a special rate for rookies, but when we got there, the manager said he had no rooms for us and couldn't say where we could find one.

"That's OK, we'll sleep in the car," Willie said.

I wasn't going to take that. "Don Shula told me we were supposed to stay here and that you have a room for us. We're either going to sleep in the lobby or you're going to give us a room." The guy was angry and belligerent, but we got a room. Willie was from the South, and blacks didn't talk to whites that way down there. I was from the North and arrogant and never really thought about the fact that the guy wasn't prepared to give me a room because I was black.

I learned a lot in my rookie year, but one thing I never learned was to back down.

CHAPTER 5

LIFE IN THE NFL

It was a learning experience on and off the field in the NFL. There were big expectations for the team going into the 1963 season, and those expectations remained high after we went 4–1 in the exhibition season. So it was quite a letdown for everyone when we lost the season opener at home, in front of more than 60,000 fans, to the New York Giants, 37–28. I caught my first NFL touchdown pass, a 32-yarder from Unitas, one of three catches I had that day.

Then we went on a three-week road trip, with away games at San Francisco, Green Bay, and Chicago. We came from behind to beat the 49ers 20–14, evening our record to 1–1. I had two more catches, and by that point in the season, the rookie from Syracuse was second in receiving yards, behind Jimmy Orr, with 110. The third week we faced the defending champions, Vince Lombardi's Packers, at Lambeau Field. We had to do so without Raymond Berry, who had dislocated his left shoulder in the San Francisco game. We couldn't afford to be short against a team like Green Bay, and it showed in a 31–20 defeat. We were now 1–2, and the grumbling over failed expectations was beginning. For my part, it appeared I was exceeding the expectations that people had for me. I caught five passes for 98 yards against the Packers, and Lombardi said I was "the best-looking rookie I've seen so far this year."

I may have been getting accolades, but our team was falling fast. We lost the following week, this time 10–3 to the Chicago Bears at Soldier Field. That put us at 1–3, and we were coming home to face the San Francisco 49ers again. With the support of the hometown fans, we bounced back to win 20–3. But even though the team got a win, I went the other way with less than my best performance. We just couldn't get on the same page. Late in the fourth quarter, when it was clear the game was won, Shula put in rookie quarterback Gary Cuozzo, who had a chance for a memorable debut. I blew it by dropping a touchdown pass from him. I let reporters know after the game that I was clearly disappointed with my performance. "I dropped too many balls today," I said. "I've just got to work on that, starting tomorrow. The one from Cuozzo . . . well, I just took my eyes off it for a second. No excuse for it."

Cuozzo was stand up about my miss after the game. "I told John to forget about that pass," he told reporters. "It could happen to anyone. Besides, I reminded him, if it weren't for you making that touchdown catch against the Washington Redskins [in an exhibition game in Norfolk, Virginia] I might not have been on the Colts team."

People were starting to take notice of me around the league. *Pro Football Illustrated* did an article after the San Francisco game declaring that I was the front-runner for NFL Rookie of the Year honors. "John Mackey looks like a cinch to give anybody a run all the way to the finish for rookie honors. The guy who beats him out will need to be a fantastic football player. . . . Mackey is almost never stopped by the first defender to grab him, and sometimes not by the second or even the third. Sometimes he slips them and sometimes he tramples them, but one way or another he usually keeps going. He needs an awful lot of tackling." When reporters asked me about the story, I answered, "If anything like that would happen, the credit would have to go to Jim Mutscheller." The attention was nice, but I had to remember I was a rookie on a team full of veterans who had already won championships, and I really hadn't proved anything yet.

We continued with a win the following week, coming from behind to beat the Lions in Detroit 25–21. With two straight wins, our record was now 3–3, and it appeared we were on our way back to a playoff season—except that we had to play Green Bay and Chicago again. We didn't fare any better the second time. The Packers beat us 34–20, and the Bears won 17–7. Both games were at home with more than 60,000 people on hand at Memorial Stadium to watch us lose. There was a point in the Green Bay game where we nearly turned it around. We had been down 20–3 and closed the gap to 20–13. Unitas sent the ball deep, which I managed to get under and catch at the Green Bay 20. I got into the end zone for a 58-yard touchdown catch, tying the game 20–20 in the fourth quarter. But that was all the scoring we did, as the Packers put the game away. Even though I was a rookie, I was developing a profile in Baltimore, and was invited to write a first-person account of the game in the *Baltimore News-Post*, an afternoon paper in the city. The following is my account of the defeat:

> Going into the game we felt this was the most important one so far. It was a "must."
>
> If we could knock over the Green Bay Packers then we would be in a great spot for pulling off one of the most surprising finishes the National Football League has ever known.
>
> All the players on the Colts felt a win yesterday would have carried us through to the title. We gave ourselves a great chance to win it. If we took this one, we would have gone all the way. We definitely felt that way.
>
> Of course, this was predicated on handling the Packers. We're still not out of the Western Division race but a realistic look tells us that a lot of things would have to happen for us to beat the Chicago Bears and the team that beat us yesterday, the Packers.
>
> But we won't quit. I know this team has too many fine men for us to resign ourselves to giving up. We're disappointed and words can't describe how badly we feel.
>
> All we can do is keep banging away, game after game, and hope that something opens up

for us. Once the game is over, I try to forget it. There's no sense in running it over and over and feeling sorry for yourself.

The Packers were like champions in all sports. They took advantage of our mistakes and we couldn't capitalize on their errors. The most important thing is winning and when you don't there's no point to trying to cry or alibi.

The only thing that means anything in the concluding analysis is what they put up on the scoreboard as the final result. Yesterday it was Green Bay 34, Baltimore 20. I thought we had them on the run when we got to a 20–20 tie in the last period but they got off the hook.

I know everybody is talking about the questionable pass-interference call that was made against Lenny Lyles as he covered Max McGee. You fans in the stands had a better look at it than I did.

I was on the sidelines and didn't have a good view of the play. My original thought was that he had made a good play, but the official had a much better angle than I did.

I have enough to worry about personally without disputing an official's call when I wasn't in position to see what happened. I saw Lyles in the locker room after the game but we didn't talk about it.

He was putting an ice pack on his shoulder and I asked him how the shoulder was feeling.

Not too good, I guess, but Lenny wasn't complaining. He's never much for making a lot of noise or commotion.

Our defense played a good game. The offense played a good game for the second half. What was wrong with us in the first half? I don't have the answer to that.

We more or less changed our mental outlook. It seemed we had more desire in the second half than the first. Why? I can't figure it out.

Coach Don Shula was upset, but he was himself. He didn't rant or rave but just put it to us bluntly that we were capable of doing a much better job. Coach Shula didn't make any changes at halftime.

We stayed with our plans but certainly executed everything a lot better in the second half than in the first. Most of the game I was blocking in tight on Willie Davis, Dan Currie, or Bill Forester.

I have this cut lip and I know I have been favoring it. Davis was coming out on me aggressively, more than I thought he would, but I believe this was because he was concerned about me coming back in to block on him.

I guess maybe I was open four or five times on patterns throughout the day and I knew that I could evade Hank Gremminger, the Packers defensive back. At least I thought I could.

Right before the touchdown play, he was playing me real close, and I felt I could go either way on him. So I told John Unitas before we huddled what I thought I could do.

On that play, the one coming up, John called it. It was a tight end option and I could either "z-out" or "z-in." I didn't fake at all. I just ran by Gremminger.

Unitas told me in practice that when I go into a fake against a defender that I lose some of my speed and that it's just as important to try to run by the halfback.

That's exactly what I tried to do. I could see the ball almost all the way, but there was a second or a fraction of a second when I didn't see it. But I picked it up in the air and told myself to "look the ball into my hands."

I couldn't comment one way or the other on the pass-interference call. But I was in the game when Unitas was called for intentionally grounding the ball. I know that Jimmy Orr was coming across in the end zone and was definitely in the area of the pattern.

I was surprised when the call was made because I felt John was justified in throwing it there. On our first touchdown, Lenny Moore ran a great pattern. And Unitas waited until the last possible second.

Just as Lenny came open, John fired. It was perfect. And it wasn't an easy completion because there was a lot of traffic between Unitas and Moore.

In the second half, when we started to roll, we were gaining confidence and there wasn't any doubt in my mind that we were going to win. But, as I said earlier, it's only the end that really has any meaning to it.

Certainly the Packers deserve credit to make the kind of showing they did. They're a top team. Give them what they earned. I'm finding out that you don't win in this league without talent.

John Roach, subbing for Bart Starr, looked like a number one quarterback to me. He turned in a good job. I thought that maybe the Packers were putting out a little "extra" for him and it just might have been true.

Jimmy Taylor runs hard and makes yardage when it's needed. But he's not a Jim Brown in my book. Marv Fleming made some brilliant receptions for the Packers. I played against him in the East-West Game and the Hula Bowl, but I didn't know he could catch like that. And there's a good reason. In both of those games, Fleming was used on defense.

In this story, I would like to thank John Unitas, Dick Bielski, Raymond Berry, and coach Jim Mutscheller for all the help they have given me in my rookie year. All the fellows have been especially kind, and I'd like to get it on the record how I feel.

I felt that in being a rookie that maybe Unitas wouldn't want to throw to me. But that was a wrong idea. He even stays out after the regular practice and works with me and tries to help me correct my errors.

Coach Mutscheller helped me with my blocking and told me things to look for when playing against certain linebackers. Raymond has showed me how to study the films and use things that you see.

Bielski has definitely helped me running pass patterns. He runs good patterns himself, so when he tells you something you can believe he knows what he's talking about.

I thought that as a rookie I would be strictly on my own. But that was wrong. All the players have tried to help me.

I hope that I can make a contribution to the future success of the Colts. And I'm hopeful I can be on some championship Colts teams because I like it here and everything about the game and pro football.

But, actually, the crowds, the excitement, and thrills come in second best. You have to win. There's just no substitute for winning.

Not exactly Pulitzer Prize material, but pretty heady stuff for a rookie—a page-one story, a remarkable turn of events for a man who once got into trouble for trying to use the bathroom in this town while passing through as a little boy. The recognition brought me a sense of satisfaction, but it was always secondary to winning. The Baltimore Colts were used to winning, and despite my page-one story, not much changed the following week when we lost to Chicago, giving us a 3–5 record. Fortunately, we didn't lose three games in a row in front of our fans, as we beat the Detroit Lions 24–21 at home, thanks in large part to a big day by Johnny U, who completed 17 of 24 passes for 376 yards and two touchdowns, including a 42-yarder that I pulled down. But there were rumblings of changes to be made to keep the momentum going, and one of those changes was to use me at running back as well as tight end. We got back to .500 the next week in a wild 37–34 victory over Minnesota in Bloomington. It was a very cold place to score so many points, and a cold place to be in the backfield, where I found myself when the game began. I had one carry for three yards, but I did catch a pass on the third play of the game, broke a couple of tackles, and ran 56 yards for a touchdown to give us the early lead.

We made it to 5–5 and still clung to hopes of postseason play. Five days later, though, football records and touchdown catches and everything else seemed trivial. Five days later, our president, John F. Kennedy, was shot and killed in Dallas, Texas. We were flying to Los Angeles to play the Rams when we learned about the assassination. We had been scheduled to leave from Baltimore, but it was fogged in, so instead we flew out of Dulles airport in suburban Virginia. When we heard the news, it got really quiet on the plane. It was devastating to anyone who could see the change that had been coming over America and feel the hope for a better day that our president brought to the country. The last thing we wanted to do two days later was to play football. But NFL commissioner Pete Rozelle refused to cancel the games that Sunday, a mistake that he was criticized for all the way to his grave. We lost 17–16. I dropped what could have been the game-winning touchdown pass when Unitas hit me on the 50-yard line with a bomb that would have resulted in an 82-yard touchdown catch. There was a lot of talk about my dropped passes, and there was some concern both inside and outside the organization about my pass-catching ability.

At this point in the season we were 5–6 and just playing for respectability. A few days after the country mourned President Kennedy with a solemn ceremony in the nation's capital, we came to Washington to play the Redskins. We were ready to play that week, and pounded Washington, 36–20, at their relatively new stadium, D.C. Stadium. Years later it would be renamed RFK Stadium, after Bobby Kennedy was shot while running for president in 1968, the same year that Dr. King was assassinated, and when our country was in flames. Unitas had another huge game in the new stadium, completing 24 of 37 passes for 355 yards and three touchdowns, and I again managed to catch one of them, a 30-yard scoring play. At 6–6, we were at least back to respectability, and we were looking forward to closing out the season with two wins at home. We beat the Vikings 41–10, and any talk about keeping me at running back ended with that game. I had my best game of the year as a tight end, catching five passes for 144 yards and two touchdowns. After the game, Shula told reporters, "I don't know how you can expect a first-year tight end to do any more. He's a great prospect." And Vikings head coach Norm Van Brocklin went out of his way to mention me as well. "That rookie tight end John Mackey is going to be a terrific football player, if he isn't already." They were hard-won touchdowns, fighting my way through tacklers to get to the end zone, running 40 yards for a 61-yard touchdown, and 20 yards on a 27-yard scoring play. In the end I had to leave the game before it was over with a painful hip pointer.

After the game, I wrote another *News-Post* article, this one spelling out my preference for tight end, although my performance on the field should have made it clear to everyone that I belonged at that position.

> There's no possible way to start the season over. If we could, I know we would certainly be a serious contender for the championship. I'm just a rookie, but I've seen enough of the league to realize that our team would be a factor.
>
> Early in the season I thought I was catching passes OK, but not blocking good enough. Then I started concentrating on the blocking and my pass receiving suffered.
>
> Right now I think maybe my receiving and blocking are close to being comparable, although there's still much to be done before I'm an established professional.
>
> I won't consider myself satisfied until every block I make is a good one, every pass that's thrown to me I catch, and every pass I get my hands on is run in for a touchdown.
>
> Sure, I'd like to be the Rookie of the Year because it would be a great honor. But I don't let my mind dwell on anything like that. I really have too much work to do.

Last Wednesday night, coach Don Shula gave me the film of the last game with the Minnesota Vikings, and I watched it closely. Raymond Berry told me it's worth studying yourself in films as well as the man you might have playing against you.

I realized, after watching the game and trying to analyze why I was dropping so many passes, that I was taking my eyes off the ball at the last second. I was so anxious to get in position to run with the ball before I even caught it that I just never had the football under control.

This past week in practice and in pregame warm-up, I really concentrated on catching every pass. And yesterday, in our 13th game of the season, was the first time all year that I didn't drop a pass.

Beating the Vikings yesterday by such an impressive score was satisfying. Let's remember we had just barely beaten them in the last game, and this was the same Vikings team that had tied the Chicago Bears, the leaders of our division.

It was good to win because our offense scored 40 points and our defense had a top day. Men like Raymond, John, Jerry Hill, Bob Boyd, and Lenny Lyles all had good individual performances.

We were glad to go ahead of .500 in our record, especially for coach Shula. All the fellows are pulling for him the way he is pulling for us. He has been fair and we all look forward to being back for a shot at the title next season.

All those injuries early in the season piled up on us, and no team could possibly have been able to win in spite of them. I know there has been some talk that I might be moved from tight end to fullback. How do I react to that?

Well, if the coaches want me to play someplace else, then I'll accept it and try to do my best. That goes if I'm playing guard or tackle or wherever they put me.

But, like I said earlier, I'm just now getting accustomed to tight end. I feel more at home where they have me now than anyplace else because I have been an end since high school.

The difference in playing tight end at Syracuse and tight end with the Colts is that they throw to you more here. In college I was primarily a blocking end, but down here they utilize me as a receiver.

Yesterday John Unitas threw me a zone pass for the first touchdown and what we call a "DQ" for the other. On the zone, John told me in the huddle to just try to get around the linebacker and hook in front of the safety.

After I got the ball I was surrounded by quite a few Vikings. I put my hand down on the ground to keep from falling and then took off running as hard as I could go.

On the "DQ" pass, I was to run a diagonal and the flanker back was to run a "Q." I was the secondary receiver, but as we broke out of the huddle, John tapped me on the seat of my pants like he might come to me with the pass. He did.

I know that R. C. Owens delivered a really good block to get me home. Unitas had the ball on target for me and I concentrated on watching it into my hands like Raymond Berry has told me so often.

Raymond has been wonderful to me. Early in the season, I had trouble getting free of the linebackers. He gave me some tips that really opened things up.

Not once this season has John Unitas gotten down on me. He never said a single word when I would drop a pass. In the Rams game in Los Angeles, I dropped the first pass and he came right back to me again.

You know, I think John was trying to work psychology on me. But he never once quit on me, and there were times when a lot of passers would have given up. Once in practice I was having a particularly bad day. The only thing John said was, "Don't worry. You drop a few and you catch a few. Don't worry." He didn't give up on me, and I know a lot of quarterbacks would have written me off the list.

There are a lot of things I admire in Unitas. He doesn't know what it is to alibi. He's also the first quarterback I've ever heard of who liked football so much that he throws a pass and runs downfield to block.

I was disappointed on the first pass I caught yesterday that I didn't get the first down. It was a delayed pattern. I left the ground to catch the pass and wasn't able to do any running with it after I had possession, or we would have picked up the first down.

What I was doing early in the year, which I'm not doing now, was running the pass patterns too fast. I was rushing everything. Sometimes I would get to the receiving area much too early. I'd have to sway into the pattern other times instead of making it look natural.

Raymond stresses to me how important it is to run out every pattern, even if you aren't supposed to have the ball thrown to you. This sets up the defensive man for when the pass does come to you. And when you run the pattern right, John has a chance to look for you if the other men are covered.

In the film I watched from our first game, I had a perfect illustration of why I didn't catch a pass. You might remember it. The ball was thrown by Gary Cuozzo, who was quarterbacking at the time.

As I went down the middle, I knew there was a man on the right, but I didn't know if there was someone on the left. So I gave it a little look to see what was doing, and I took my eye off the ball. Consequently, I didn't catch it at all.

In running with the ball, I try to maintain my balance by hitting the tackler before he hits me. In other words, I try to deliver the thrust at the instant of contact.

Almost all the players on the team have endeavored to help me. I mentioned some of their names earlier, but I don't think I brought up George Preas or Gino Marchetti. George has helped me blocking on the end and given me some valuable suggestions. And it was something Gino said that has stayed with me. He pointed out that it really wasn't doing the job if you wanted to unload on the man playing against you if it was going to slow you down or prevent you from doing the job for the team.

I can best point this out by saying that Gino told me he never tries to give the man playing against him a physical beating. He much prefers to try to get on the passer and do the job there—where it really counts for the team.

I'm sorry the season isn't just starting because I'm only now getting the picture.

The picture for the Baltimore Colts going into the final game was pride. We were playing for pride, and we managed to avenge our earlier loss to the Rams in Los Angeles with a 19–16 win at home to close the season with an 8–6 record. It was a disappointing season for the team, but for me it was a successful debut. I became an impact player on a team with a number of other impact players, finishing fourth in receiving on the team, with 35 catches for 726 yards, a team-leading 20.7 yard-per-catch average, and seven touchdowns, which was also the most among the receivers. I ran back nine kickoffs for 271 yards, a 30.1 average, which led the team. I was one of five Colts selected to play in the Pro Bowl and was the only rookie to be picked for the game. It was a great honor, one I was very proud of, particularly to be picked with Unitas, Berry, Parker, and Marchetti. (Gino announced that he would retire after this game, concluding 12 seasons in pro football. He would later be inducted into the Hall of Fame.) It was also a satisfying moment for me because Sylvia and I got married and spent our honeymoon there in Los Angeles.

I wasn't named Rookie of the Year. There were some who thought I should have won the award—one person in particular. "We felt he should have been Rookie of the Year," Shula said after the season ended. "Besides being a real threat as a receiver, he played a part in bringing our running game up from an average gain of 3.5 yards per try in 1962 to 4.1 yards last season. And we scored seven touchdowns with two goal-line plays in which John blocked in the defensive end."

It wasn't Rookie of the Year, but that sort of ringing endorsement from your coach after your first season in the NFL is a pretty good reward. It shows that you have become a professional, someone the team trusts and relies on. Later in my career, I would find out that that wouldn't be enough, and that trust wasn't a two-way street. But for now, things were pretty good for me. I was an NFL Pro Bowl tight end, catching passes from the great John Unitas. I got a job with WEBB in Baltimore doing on-air work and public relations. I had a lovely wife, Sylvia, who was building a life for us away from the field. And by the end of the season, I had a brand-new daughter—Lisa, one of the joys of my full life.

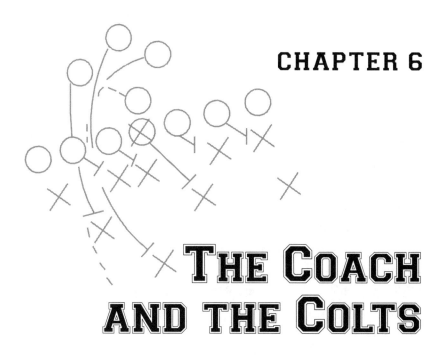

CHAPTER 6

THE COACH AND THE COLTS

Going into my second season I was feeling much more confident about my role on the team, and we were feeling very good about our chances to get back to championship form for the 1964 season. We had seen enough last year on the field to know that we had the ingredients to win, and we felt particularly good about our coach.

Don Shula was a big unknown the year before, a rookie coach and the youngest in the history of the league. But he showed us that he knew the game and was willing to listen and learn from the team. I saw him change every year that he was in Baltimore. He got better and better at his job. If I went to Shula and said, "Don, I think I can do this," he would try to work it in. It was always a two-way communication.

Here is an example of how Shula worked: he would call the first two or three plays of every game, but I couldn't understand why he did it. I now know he was trying to set the defense, to find out what they were going to give him in certain situations. He had the spotters upstairs tell him. He would give different looks to see how the other team would adjust to them.

But at the time I felt we were wasting plays. So one day before we played the Rams, I said to Shula, "Coach, why don't we just go deep on the first play? I think I can beat my man, Eddie Meader, on the first play. I can split out, get around Jack Pardee, and run the option pass. We can go for six on the first play."

Shula looked at me and said, "If you spent as much time playing tight end as you do coaching, then you'd probably be a better tight end." It was embarrassing and it made me mad because he had never come down on me like that before. I was thinking, "Who the hell does he think he is?" Part of my pregame ritual was to never eat a meal before a game. My hunger would put me in a bad mood and get me ready to play. So I was already angry when Shula brushed me off, and his response only made it worse. I told Willie Richardson, "That son of a bitch, who the hell does he think he is?" I was nearly crazy.

When we got on the bus to go to the game, I wouldn't even look at him. I wanted to win, he wanted to win. Why the hell was he coming down on me? All I wanted to do was help him by going for the deep one on the first play. We went into the locker room, got dressed, and went out onto the field for warm-ups. I still didn't look at him, and he had to know that I was mad.

When he called everybody together before the game, instead of being the guy in the middle, like I usually was, all pumped up and yelling, "We're ready to go," I was in the back of the pack. Shula said to us, "Change the first play. Tight end option to Mackey on one. He says he's going to bring us six." I couldn't believe it! My heart went from my chest down to my feet and back up to my throat. I kept thinking to myself, "I've got to do it, I've got to do it, I can't mess it up." On the first play I flew down the field and, like clockwork, grabbed the pass for an 86-yard touchdown. I ran to the sideline and Shula gave me a big hug. "I didn't give you too much time to think about it, did I?" And he was right. I'd have been thinking about it for hours if he had given me the OK right away, and I probably would have messed it up.

Shula was an excellent coach. He taught us to do everything we could to take advantage of and find the weakness in the players we were going up against. He also told us that you must go back and study yourself to find your own weaknesses because you have to assume that the guy playing against you is thinking the same way.

Shula and his coaching staff gave the impression that they thought of everything, and what they didn't think of, the players were expected to. We were taught to think out there and to improvise when the opportunity was there.

A good example was timeouts. Shula would kill you if you wasted a timeout. Our two-minute drill was so good and we had so much confidence with Johnny U running it that we made damn sure we had three timeouts to use when the two-minute warning came. To save timeouts, I was the designated injury. The tight end would fake an injury to stop the clock and save timeouts late in the game. The backup tight end would stand right next to Shula on the sideline. Since a player has to leave the field of play when he's injured, the clock is automatically stopped. The backup tight end can come in with two more plays. We used strategies like this and didn't waste any time. We always knew who was going to call timeouts, too: either the center or the quarterback. If the quarterback was knocked down and under a pile, then the center made the call.

We were so prepared for game situations it was automatic. Not only did I know what the line was doing, but I knew what the guys behind me were doing as well. Everything was a thinking situation, and everyone knew what everyone else was doing. If I ran a pass pattern, I knew that if I ran too close to Jimmy Orr or Raymond Berry, all three of us could adjust because we were taught that the three of us should never be in the same area. So if I gave an outside move and broke to the inside, but I should have broken to the outside, Raymond would automatically give an inside move and break to the outside to open up the area so Unitas could read it. Our philosophy was to think our way to solutions. As a result, we always believed we could win because we were smarter than the other team. We could win in the last few minutes, we could win in the beginning of the game. We didn't *always* win, but we felt like we could. After all, I would be in the huddle and look around to see Johnny Unitas, Raymond Berry, Lenny Moore, Jimmy Orr, and the rest of our players, and I could just feel that we were in control. Then I looked to the bench in a tough situation and knew that Shula had thought it out. We had a lot of confidence in him, and we knew beyond a doubt that Shula wanted to win. We knew that everything he was doing was geared to winning. He was the type of coach that, if we were losing, would get quieter and more analytical. But if we were ahead, he would

yell more because he didn't want a letdown. He would do anything to make sure we stayed up. If we were winning at halftime, he would tell us, "You should be ahead by 100 points,"
when we were up by 20 or so. "What kind of team are you?
You're laying down." An athlete has a tendency to coast when
he has a big lead, especially in football. The natural reaction is,
"This game is won. I don't want to get hurt now. I'll gear down
and be ready for next week." The moment you do that, you
might find that you can't gear down and then gear right back
up. And if they come back on you while you're geared down,
it's tough to turn things around. Shula was always working to
prevent this complacency from taking hold.

Shula could read the reactions of players, for the most part,
and when he said I would have spent too much time analyzing
and worrying about the play I had proposed before the Rams
game, he was right. I tried to be a thinking man's player and
break down and analyze the game like a coach. Playing with
the likes of Raymond Berry, it was hard not to. Raymond had
a huge influence on our team. He used to count the steps and
chart the athletes he played against to make sure he knew
everything they were doing, right or wrong. He would study
how to get them on the wrong foot and how to get open around
them. Raymond probably influenced Shula just as much. He
was a hard worker. That work ethic was something all of us
learned. You can't just do it on the field for an hour and a half.
I learned that you've got to stay on the field for the extra time
it takes to get that special coordination between you and the
quarterback, when he and you are working on something specific that you want to do. Raymond was a great on-field coach,
and it wasn't surprising that he went on to have success as an

NFL head coach. (He led the Patriots to the 1985 AFC championship, but they were pummeled by the Chicago Bears in the Super Bowl.)

In that kind of atmosphere, it was hard not to constantly think about the game and ways to break it down. I even went so far as to give character traits to the positions. Here's my football lesson and the way I saw our roles on the field.

Offensive linemen are like stockbrokers, three-piece-suit guys. Sane, honest family men. Defensive linemen, on the other hand, are wild men—Hell's Angels, outlaws. They don't know how to put on a shirt and tie. Linebackers are simply crazy.

The halfback is Hope, and the fullback is Faith. The halfback is usually fast, a game-breaker, very fluid and very loose. He's also got a tremendous amount of confidence and cockiness. He's got to believe that he can go 90 or 100 yards on one play. He's got to believe that he can outrun everyone else. If you give him the ball, he can go all the way. He is a thoroughbred. The fullback, on the other hand, is the plow horse. He picks up small but hard yards. He blocks for the other guy. Now with today's offenses, these roles may change, depending on the player, but the essence of their characters still remains—Hope and Faith.

The quarterback is the Leader, for obvious reasons. He has to be. But one of the more intriguing positions on the field is center. For me, the center represents Courage. I've always thought it took a hell of a lot of courage to put your head down, look between your legs, and send the ball back to the quarterback when you have someone like Dick Butkus standing over you. It's an important job because the first part of any play is to get the ball into the quarterback's hands, otherwise the rest of it doesn't happen.

On either side of the center are the two guards, and they are called Agility. They are the guys who stand in there and block to protect the quarterback, but they are also agile enough to pull out to either side to clear the way for the running back.

The tackles are Strength. Pure strength, weighing 300 pounds and anchoring the line. Nothing is going around the tackle. He's going to wipe everyone out.

The tight end is Determination. He's determined to get off the ball. He's determined to clear out the line. He's determined to catch the ball. He's determined to get the middle linebacker.

The tight end is a little crazy, too, sort of like a middle linebacker. He has to be very aggressive. He's hit on every play. There is a linebacker on the other side who is taught to not let the tight end off the line of scrimmage. There is a defensive back who, once the linebacker lets go, plays in tight. If the defense is coming up to block on a running pass pattern, the tight end has to stick close and knock the ball down. He's got to jam the defense if it's coming in too fast, slow him down, knock him off the pattern. If the tight end releases inside, there's a middle linebacker who wants to knock him on his behind. He knows he's going to get hit on every play. If he's not trying to catch the ball, he's trying to control someone else so that his teammates can get open—like I said, the tight end is Determination and a little bit Crazy.

The flankers—the end split from the line—are Perseverance. Many times they are not that big, and they've got to go out there and run their patterns on every play. And when I played, it was bump-and-run, so they had to get back up and run another play. They had to persevere.

When you put it all together, you have one Leader, the quarterback, with Courage in the middle and Agility on either side of him. Then Strength, Determination, and Perseverance are down the line, with Faith and Hope in the backfield.

I never really thought about the defensive personalities as in-depth as I did the offensive players, in part because I was more familiar with offense, and also because I was so confident going against defensive players. I believed I could block a defensive lineman, no matter how big he was or how good he was, because as the offensive player I knew I had the advantage—I knew what I was going to do, and he had to figure it out. I might have only a half-second advantage, but that was usually good enough for me. If I got off on the count, that was it, there was nothing they could do about it.

That sounds pretty cocky, but I was simply confident in my abilities and determination—when I was healthy. In my second year as a pro I needed a lot of those qualities—faith, hope, perseverance, determination, and a few others, too. It went south for me during an exhibition game in Hershey, Pennsylvania, against the Philadelphia Eagles. The field had poor lighting. The play was a tight end option. I made my inside move and went right to the posts, and Unitas threw the ball directly overhead. That's the most difficult pass to catch because you can't get an angle on it. I was running upfield as fast as I could, looking directly over my head, and then BOOM! I ran right into the goal post. I was out of it. Everyone was surprised when I got up and walked over to the wrong huddle. Sylvia was in Washington, so someone drove me to her mother's house after the game. I ate dinner, but I couldn't remember Sylvia's name. It took about two days before I got my memory back. That was the hardest I ever got hit, but there was another one later that year that was a close second.

I hurt from the collision in Hershey for most of the season. The contusions in my thigh never really healed. I developed calcium deposits, and I wasn't able to practice during the season. I was a one-legged player for most of the time and wound up favoring my other leg, which didn't help. I don't believe you are a real pro unless you can play when you're hurt, so I wasn't about to sit down. But it was a new thing for me; I had never really been hurt before, not like this, and had to play through it like I did. I didn't fully recover until the last game of the regular season. Facing the Washington Redskins, with the score tied 17–17 late in the third quarter, I took a pass from Unitas and ran it in for a 22-yard touchdown. The pass I caught against Washington was only my second touchdown of the season, and I caught just 22 passes for 406 yards that year. I didn't have the part of the game that I needed to be a successful tight end—the explosion after catching the ball, the ability to break tackles and knock people over. For most of the season, blocking was the only way I could help the team. I felt much better, though, after the season finale. We certainly felt better as a team, and for good reason—our season wasn't over yet.

The Baltimore Colts had been the league's dominant team that year. We lost the season opener at Minnesota against the Vikings, 34–24, but never looked back after that. We reeled off 11 straight wins, starting with a hard-fought 21–20 win over the Green Bay Packers at Lambeau Field. Then we came home and broke out the big stick against the defending-champion Chicago Bears, destroying them 52–0.

But speaking of destroyed, I was leveled in that blowout against Chicago by a monster of a man, defensive end Doug Atkins. At 6'9" and 280 pounds, Atkins, at that time, was larger than life. On one play, Shula had me flare out of the backfield. I was looking back in case Unitas threw the ball, and I got clotheslined by Atkins. It never would have happened if I had been playing from the tight end position. Coming out of the backfield, I wasn't even thinking about the clothesline. After he hit me, you would have thought I was walking on hot coals. Atkins rang my bell. I was weaving around like a drunk and wobbled back to the bench. Everyone had a laugh about it on Monday when we watched the game films. They jokingly offered me advice, like "Watch where you're going," and "Keep your head down," and stuff like that.

The Bears had plenty of defensive guys on the field that you had to worry about, and, of course, the main one was middle linebacker Dick Butkus, who joined them the following season. It's funny; Dick had two personalities. He was one of the nicest guys you would ever want to meet off the field. But when he was on the field, he lived to knock your block off. He always went for the football and didn't like to be blocked, and he would let you know it. He would say things like, "Who the hell do you think you are blocking me? Get out of my way!" He would tackle the offensive guards as they pulled. He hit anything in an opposition jersey that was moving. We had a 34-trap play where the tight end splits out and blocks the middle linebacker from the blind side just as he's stepping up to meet the fullback head-on. We never could block Butkus on that play because he never came down the line to the four-hole. He went right through the center and ran down the back from behind. He liked to go right over the center because he knew the guy was preoccupied with another task—snapping the ball. Butkus was allowed to roam behind the line. He had a natural instinct for the ball. I also know that he watched the quarterback's eyes. For a couple of years we tried to figure out why he went in a certain direction when every linebacker in that same situation did something completely different. And we knew that the middle linebacker's job was to follow the fullback. Butkus would do that sometimes, but other times he would not. Unitas finally figured it out for us. He saw that Butkus was watching his eyes and said, "I'm going to test this." Unitas did just that in a game against Butkus when he looked to the left but threw a little pop pass to the right, a quick release inside and then dump to the tight end, and we fooled Butkus—at least that time.

The wins kept coming—35–20 against the Rams; 47–27 over the Cardinals; another close win, 24–21, over the Packers; 34–0 against the Lions; 37–7 over the 49ers; 40–24 against the Bears in Chicago; 17–14 over the Vikings, avenging our opening loss to them; 24–7 over the Rams; and 14–3 against the 49ers. I have to admit, the games against the 49ers were particularly difficult for me because it meant I had to go up against the guy who gave me the most trouble in the league— linebacker Dave Wilcox. He was the most physical guy I played against in the NFL, and I played against a lot of tough guys. When he first came into the league, I thought I could intimidate him. I went off and stuck him pretty good. I stood up in his face and made him bite his tongue. I thought I took care of him pretty good. Shula was on the sideline going crazy because I got called for an offside penalty, but Unitas was in the huddle laughing and said, "Hey, now that you've softened him up, let's

99

run at him." We ran at him, all right. To my amazement, he picked me up by my shoulder pads and threw me back into Unitas for a 10-yard loss. Suddenly it was third down with about 20 yards to go for the first down, and we had problems. Shula was still steaming, and I was embarrassed. I went back to the huddle and told Unitas, "Let's run it again."

Unitas yelled back, "Shut up! Forget it! We're going to leave that guy alone." Wilcox wound up intimidating me. I had never been handled like that before. For a spell, every time we played the 49ers, I thought Dave Wilcox would pound my neck down between my shoulders. I was at a loss about what to do, so I asked our coach-on-the-field, Raymond Berry, for help. He studied the films for several days and then came to me and said, "You line up so close to your tackle that you think he'll be able to help you. He can't. If you split out five yards, it's a natural split, and you can stay out there and fight with Dave Wilcox. It will create a more natural hole for Matte or Moore to run through. I did it, and it worked. Then the San Francisco coaches started getting on Wilcox to get on me, and he came in closer on the line. Then I got the inside angle on him and he wasn't a problem anymore. But there was a time when I thought he was really going to knock my block off.

After the win over the 49ers, we were smoking, with an 11–1 record. We were flying a little too high, I guess. We lost 31–14, at home of all places, to Detroit, a team we had shut out earlier in the season. It was our only home loss. We bounced back with the victory over Washington to finish the year, and what a great offensive year it had been.

We scored 428 points in 14 games, more than 200 points better than what we allowed (225 points). Unitas threw for 2,824 yards and 19 touchdowns, but our bread and butter that year was the running game—the part of the offense where I could still contribute strongly. We averaged nearly 30 yards more per game than we had the year before, running for an average of 143.4 yards per game and 2,007 for the season. The receivers were spread out, with seven pulling down 10 or more passes. Raymond Berry led the team with 43 catches for 663 yards, followed by Jimmy Orr with 40 catches for 867 yards. I was third on the team again with 22 catches for 406 yards, but we had a number of others step up to fill in where I had dropped off. Lenny Moore caught 21 passes for 472 yards, and Jerry Hill caught 14 passes for 113 yards. Running back Tony Lorick caught 11 passes for 164 yards, and Tom Matte finished with 10 catches for 169 yards.

Oh, yeah, there was one player who caught just one pass for one yard, but everyone remembers him. Anyone who ever played with Joe Don Looney remembers him, but for all the wrong reasons. He was about the strangest man who ever walked on the football field, a player with great physical gifts that kept teams interested in him even when he wore out his welcome in one city after another. He spent the 1964 season with the Colts, and I remember that he only ran back a few kickoffs, which drove the coaches crazy. He once punted a ball high and deep during practice, as high and as deep as I've ever seen a punt go. He declared out loud to everyone watching, "How'd you like that one, God?" He was drafted by the New York Giants in 1964 but was soon traded to the Colts after missing training camp and outright refusing to learn plays. He wasn't in Baltimore for long, and then went on to Detroit and Washington and finally out of the league. While he was in

Detroit, the coach, Harry Gilmer, told Looney to bring a play into the huddle. Looney refused, and left the team at halftime. "If he wanted a messenger, he should have called Western Union," Looney said afterward. Once Looney skipped practice during training camp and linebacker Joe Schmidt found him in the dorm room. "You ought to come to practice," Schmidt told Looney. "You're part of the team. You'll get fined."

Looney answered, "Joe, how long have you been doing this, going to practice every day?"

Schmidt told him 14 years, to which Looney replied, "Joe, you ought to take a day off once in a while." That concept was so foreign to me. Looney wasted his God-given talent, but he was a tormented man. He later joined up with a guru, or something like that, and died a young man.

Even with Joe Don Looney and all of the craziness that year, we not only succeeded but dominated, winning the Western Conference title. All that was left between us and the NFL championship were the Eastern Conference champions—the Cleveland Browns, who had a one-man running game that dwarfed all others.

Jim Brown led Cleveland to the conference title, and, for me, a chance to play against my boyhood idol was something special. This was the player I grew up watching on Long Island, the player I followed in winning the Thorp award as the outstanding high school player on Long Island, the player I followed to Syracuse. Now Jim Brown was all that stood between the Colts and an NFL title. It turned out he was more than enough, and he had a lot of help when the Browns crushed us, 27–0, in Cleveland before a wild crowd of nearly 80,000 fans.

It was a crazy game—actually two games in one. The first half ended in a 0–0 tie, and there was no indication that it would wind up anything other than a close game, perhaps with one score making the difference. But we came out of the locker room flat, and the Browns took advantage of it by scoring 17 points. We were finished. Then it turned into a disaster. Browns quarterback Frank Ryan completed 11 of 18 passes for 206 yards and three touchdowns, all to Gary Collins, for 18, 42, and 51 yards. Jim Brown did his usual damage on the ground, rushing for 114 yards on 27 carries. On our side of the ball, it was a breakdown offensively. Unitas had trouble with the wind at Municipal Stadium and threw for just 95 yards, with 12 completions in 20 attempts and two interceptions. Lenny Moore ran for just 40 yards, Jerry Hill had 31 yards rushing, and the running game was so bad that Unitas wound up being our third best ball carrier, with six carries for 30 yards. Raymond Berry caught three passes for 38 yards, Jimmy Orr two for 31, and Tony Lorick had three catches for just 18 yards. That was about the extent of our offense in the NFL championship game. Me? I had one catch for two yards. Cleveland coach Paul Brown challenged us at seven yards. Our pass routes, our receivers in the secondary . . . everything was thrown off. We should have been running our pass patterns deeper, but they challenged us at every play.

It was hard for me because we were so close to being NFL champions in just my second year. Getting a taste of it, I wanted to win one now more than ever, and I thought we would get another chance in 1965. It seemed like it would be a repeat of 1964. We won the opener at home against Minnesota, 35–16, then lost the next week to the Packers, 20–17, at

County Stadium in Milwaukee. Then we went on another win streak—eight straight, starting with a 27–24 victory over the 49ers at home and ending with a 34–24 win against Philadelphia at home. We entered the 11th week with a 9–1 record, but then we hit a rough spot. We played to a 24–24 tie against the Lions in Detroit, and then lost two straight, 13–0 to Chicago and 42–27 to Green Bay, both at home. They were devastating losses for us that went beyond the scoreboard. Unitas had been battling injuries all year, and he finally went down for good that season with a torn ligament and cartilage damage in the loss to the Bears. Then backup quarterback Gary Cuozzo separated his shoulder in the next week's loss to the Packers. We went into the final game of the season, against the Rams, with Tom Matte, a halfback, playing quarterback. He had been a quarterback at Ohio State in college, but that simply meant handing the ball off under Woody Hayes' offense. Matte handled the job well, not making any mistakes and rushing for 90 yards from the quarterback position. He had the plays written on his wristbands. I had a big catch—a 68-yard touchdown—but not from Matte. It came from the emergency quarterback we brought into camp just the day before, Ed Brown. With a 10–3–1 record, now we would have to play the Packers for the second time in three weeks in a playoff for the Western Conference title. We fell short again, losing 13–10 in overtime in Green Bay in a hard-fought game. It certainly wasn't like the year before, when we collapsed against Cleveland (even though we had every reason to collapse this time). Shula went with Matte at quarterback. Ironically, the Packers didn't have their great quarterback either, as Bart Starr was injured and could not play. But at least they had an NFL quarterback, their backup,

Zeke Bratkowski. Even with the deck stacked against us, we should have won the game—really. I'm not saying we should have won the game but blew it. I'm saying we should have had that victory but the referees blew it, as if we needed more things to go wrong for us.

We got on the board first, just 21 seconds into the game, when Don Shinnick scooped up Bill Anderson's fumble and ran in 25 yards for a score, putting us ahead 7–0. We added three points to that lead in the second quarter with a field goal by Lou Michaels, and went into the locker room at halftime with a 10–0 lead—a remarkable turn of events, considering we had our halfback playing quarterback against a team like the Packers. It caught up with us in the second half, but not by much. The Packers scored in the third quarter on a one-yard run by Paul Hornung. Then came the play that robbed us of a remarkable victory. As time was running out, the Packers, down 10–7, moved the ball into position for a 22-yard field-goal attempt by Don Chandler. It went wide right. Nearly everyone on the field saw it go wide right. Chandler knew it had gone wide right. You could see he knew he missed it as he walked about looking dejected. It was a shock to him and everyone else when official Jim Tunney called the kick good, which tied the game at 10–10. Replays show that the kick sailed wide right, but that did us no good. So the game went into overtime, and this time we weren't the Colts of sudden death victory like the team was back in 1958, in that historic game against the New York Giants. We lost when Chandler hit a 25-yard field goal to win. To look at the numbers, it was amazing we were even there to compete, but our defense allowed us to do that. Bratkowski completed 22 of 39 passes for 248 yards but had no touchdowns and two interceptions. His longest completion was just 16 yards. Fullback Jim Taylor had only 60 yards rushing on 23 carries, and Hornung had 33 yards on 10 carries. For us, Matte managed to complete 5 of 12 passes for 40 yards, with no interceptions. I caught three of those passes for 25 yards, but most of our offense was on the ground. Matte rushed for 57 yards on 17 carries, Jerry Hill had 57 yards on 16 carries, and Lenny Moore had 33 yards on 12 carries. We had overcome so much to compete in that game, and to have it pulled out from under us because of a bad call broke our hearts. Because of that bad call, the NFL decided to place two officials under the goal posts on field-goal tries and also made the goal posts 10 feet higher.

Overall, I rebounded in 1965 to have a good season, primarily because I was healthy much of the time. I caught 40 passes for 814 yards, scored seven touchdowns, and led the team with a 20.4 yard-per-catch average. Raymond Berry led the team with 58 catches for 739 yards, and Jimmy Orr was second with 45 catches for 847 yards. Johnny U completed 164 out of 282 passes for 2,530 yards and 23 touchdowns, and his backup, Cuozzo, completed 54 of 105 passes for 7 touchdowns.

The 1966 season didn't start out very well, at least not from the Colts' perspective. I had no problems with the situation because I was just standing up for what I believed was right, and I was setting the tone, in my fourth year, for the way the organization would have to deal with me. I came to camp without a contract, and when it appeared they were not going to take me seriously, I simply left. I told reporters, "I shouldn't be practicing without a contract. When I came to camp, I came to play. I didn't want to talk contract. I have a one-track mind, and I can't concentrate on football and salary at the same time. I'll never come to camp without a contract again." So I left. I went down to Chesapeake Bay and took the boat I owned out on the water so they couldn't come out to see me. They would have to rent a boat first. The problem I had was negotiating with Don Kellett, the general manager. Every time I asked him for something, he would say, "I can't do that. I can't do that." I was looking to make $35,000 that year. I had a clause in my contract that stated that Rosenbloom was the only one who could negotiate my contract. So I told Shula I was leaving because I couldn't talk to Kellett, I had to talk to Rosenbloom. What really got me mad was, right after a hard practice, when we were going up the hill, Kellett said, "I want to see you in my room." I got dressed and went to his room, and it had air-conditioning. We didn't have air-conditioning, and we were the ones who were busting our humps out there in the hot summer sun. That really got me angry. Then he said, "I can't give you what you want."

"That ends the conversation," I said.

I went to Shula's room and told him, "I'm going home."

"Don't go home," Shula said. "You'll hurt the club."

"Look, Carroll Rosenbloom said he would be here two days ago, and he never showed up," I said. "I know he's supposed to come here tomorrow, but I'll be at home."

"I don't blame you," Shula said. "But as a coach, I don't want you to go. But I want you to know that if you leave, when you come back, you'll still be my tight end."

As I walked out, I ran into Jimmy Orr, and he asked me, "Where are you going?"

I said, "I'm going home."

"Give me five minutes," Jimmy said. "I'll be joining you." He went in to see Kellett, came out, went in to see Shula, and the both of us left camp together.

Rosenbloom showed up the next day, but we were long gone. He sent his son Steve out after me. I was told to be in Rosenbloom's office at 3:00 P.M. the following day. I was there waiting and waiting and waiting. Finally, at 9:00 P.M. the owner strolled in just as I was walking out.

"Where's my boy going?" he asked.

We went inside his office, and he said to me, "Do you want something to drink? But we can't have any alcoholic beverages now, can we," wagging his finger at me like a schoolmarm. He was acting crazy, and then he made a wrong move—he called my wife, Sylvia. It was like I was in the principal's office. "Sylvia? How's the bride?" Rosenbloom asked. "What are we going to do with him?"

Sylvia knew she couldn't talk for me, and she cut the conversation short. "I can't discuss this," she said. "Anything you want to discuss, you'll have to talk to John about it." Rosenbloom had a very paternalistic attitude, and not always in a good way. Finally we reached a deal for 1966, and I had accomplished my mission—to make sure that Rosenbloom knew that he had to deal with me.

We had gotten so close to winning a championship in 1964, and, just like in 1965, we were chomping at the bit to get back and complete what we had missed out on in the two previous seasons. We got off to a rocky start, losing the season opener to the Packers, 24–3, in Milwaukee. Then, as before, we went on a winning spree, taking seven of our next eight games. We beat the Vikings, 38–23, in Minnesota, and then won our home

opener, a 36–14 victory over San Francisco. We lost the following week to the Bears in Chicago, 27–17, but bounced back
with wins over Detroit (45–17), Minnesota (20–17), Los
Angeles (17–3), Washington (37–10), and the Atlanta Falcons
(19–7). We were 7–2, and it looked as if we were on our way
to another Western Conference title. But we couldn't keep up
the momentum and lost three of our last five games. We lost
two straight, to Detroit (20–14) and the Rams (23–7). We finished the regular season with a win over Chicago (21–16),
another loss to Green Bay (14–10), and a victory over the 49ers
in San Francisco (30–14), winding up with a disappointing
9–5 record and a ticket to the runner-up bowl against
Philadelphia in Miami, which we won 20–14.

We had some problems offensively. Unitas had 22 touchdown passes, but also threw 24 interceptions. It seemed like we
had taken a step back. But I had my best season yet, finishing
second on the team in receptions, with 50 catches for 829 yards
and nine touchdowns, and I made the Pro Bowl for the second
time in my four-year career. Two of my better games came,
unfortunately, when we lost. In our first game against the
Bears, I caught a 10-yard pass from Unitas on our own 19-yard
line. I headed down the field, and there was safety Ritchie
Petitbon in my way. I knew from facing him before that he
would stand his ground and try to force me into making a
move. I slowed up for a second, bent over, and came up with
my right arm and right knee as he went to hit me. He went up
into the air and flew backward. Waiting for me next was Mr.
Monster-of-the-Midway himself, Butkus. I faked left, went
right, and left Butkus behind. Then I outran safety Roosevelt
Taylor into the end zone for a 79-yard touchdown. Six games

later, in a loss to the Lions in Detroit, I took a five-yard pass from Cuozzo on our 39-yard line. Dick LeBeau tried to bring me down, but I ran over him and bounced off nearly the entire Lions defense, even LeBeau for a second time, as he got up and tried to bring me down again. I shed him, and when all was said and done, I had knocked down about seven Detroit defenders on the way to the end zone. After the game, Matte said it was "the greatest individual effort I've ever witnessed," and center Dick Szymanski said, "I've never seen a run that even approached it." The shame was that both efforts came in losses, which was the bottom line—winning and losing. That was always the driving force for the Baltimore Colts during my time there, and in the next few years to come, I would experience the best and worst of both worlds. I would have never had such experiences, though, if it weren't for the chance to play with the greatest quarterback in the history of the NFL—my quarterback, Johnny Unitas.

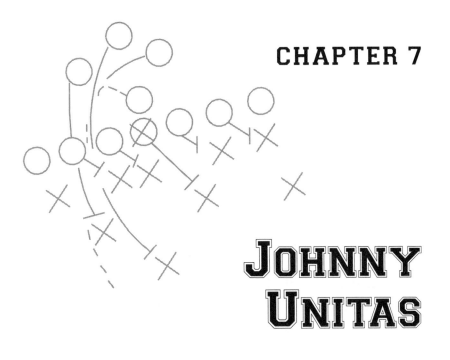

CHAPTER 7

JOHNNY UNITAS

It is impossible to write the story of my life in football without having a big part of it be about Johnny Unitas. Anyone who played with him during the Colts' glory years would have to say the same thing. He was a once-in-a-lifetime teammate, and we knew it. He was the greatest quarterback to ever play the game. He was the first quarterback to throw for more than 40,000 yards over his 18-year career. He completed 2,830 of 5,186 passes, and threw 290 touchdowns. When he retired after the 1973 season, Unitas held 22 NFL records. He was the league's Most Valuable Player in 1964 and 1967 and played in 10 Pro Bowls. When the NFL had its 50th anniversary in 1969, Unitas was voted the greatest quarterback of all time, and when the NFL's All-Time team was selected in 2000, Unitas was named the quarterback. Johnny Unitas was my quarterback, and he will always be my quarterback.

"He was one of the toughest competitors I've ever known and overcame tremendous odds to become one of the greatest passers in NFL history," Don Shula said of his quarterback from 1963 to 1969.

Tremendous odds is right. Unitas was not an anointed star coming out of college. He was an outstanding quarterback at Louisville, but he was cut by the Pittsburgh Steelers in 1955. He spent that year playing semipro football and working construction, and, after Weeb Ewbank received a letter from a fan who had seen Unitas play on the semipro team, the Colts signed him to be a backup quarterback in 1956. He quickly earned the starting job, and the legend began.

More important to me, Johnny Unitas was an honest man with a good heart. Like I've said before, being in the huddle with Johnny Unitas was like being in the huddle with God. That's why his sudden death at the age of 69 hit me and so many of the old Colts very hard. We had a bond that had lasted long after football, and it wasn't something that needed to be nurtured. It was there whether we saw each other once a year or once every five years.

John wasn't a man of many words, and now that he is gone, the words he did speak seem more precious and important than ever. Here are excerpts from an interview conducted after his playing days were over.

On Owners

Owners like Gene Klein and Bob Irsay—they don't belong in the NFL. The game is a one-way street for the owners.

They don't take care of the players, and I'm glad to see players now get their pound of flesh from the owners, because it is the players who are the people who make the game and the teams.

On the Departure of the Colts from Baltimore

It devastates the feelings of the people. It devastates the people who manage the city, the mayor, and the governor because it takes away a tremendous amount of money. And it keeps on multiplying and multiplying and it continues on. It has a tremendous effect on the people who go to the games on Sunday and consider that to be their one big day of the week, like this town did. Because this was a blue-collar town, they used to hold 10,000 tickets for open window sale on Saturday or during the week. They would reserve those tickets because they already had 40,000 tickets sold. Those other 10,000 tickets would be for the people who couldn't afford to buy season tickets or for those who worked shift work and couldn't always get to a game. Professional football was a big thing here. Go out and have a good time, and on Monday, if we won, everyone talked about that football game right up to the next Saturday. If we lost, it was a real pain in the ass to go to work because everyone would be screaming and moaning that Unitas didn't do this or that, or Mackey dropped this pass, or someone didn't kick a field goal. But they were always behind us 100 percent.

On Recognition and Appreciation by the Fans

I have a lot of people who come up to me and say, "Thanks for the entertainment you provided over the years. There ain't ever going to be anything like you guys again." That's a great feeling to have people come up and say that. It's nice for people to remember.

On Today's Football Players

There's no togetherness. There is no camaraderie off the field because their main interest is in money. We didn't have that interest, because we didn't make any money. My first contract was for $7,000. George Shaw was playing ahead of me. He was a bonus choice in 1955. He had a two-year contract at $17,500. It took me three years before I got up to that. I thought $7,000 was all the money there was in the world. I didn't know any different.

After we won the title in 1958 and 1959, I went to Kellett [Don Kellett, the Colts general manager]. He screamed at me, "What do you want?" I told him I wanted a raise to $25,000, and he said he couldn't talk to me, that I had to talk to Carroll Rosenbloom. So we went to Rosenbloom. He had a suite at the Belvedere Hotel. We went into his office, and he asked me, "John, what seems to be the problem between you and Don?"

"We don't have a problem, Mr. Rosenbloom," I said. "I think Mr. Kellett's got the problem. I asked him for $25,000 and he said he couldn't talk to me, and I had to talk to you. So here I came."

Rosenbloom said, "John, guys who have played in this league for 10 years don't make $25,000."

"Wait a minute," I said. "Do you pay your players on the amount of time spent in the league or their ability to do the job?" Rosenbloom looked over at Kellett and said, "I think he's got you." I got my money.

More on Salaries

The biggest problem for players back then was the lack of willingness to talk to each other about salaries. The last thing the general manager said to you after you signed was, "Remember, this is between us. Don't talk to the newspapers. Don't talk to anybody else about what you make."

I had a thing set up one year with Y. A. Tittle, myself, and Jim Brown. It was a year when I was the MVP, and Y.A. and Jimmy finished right behind me. I said to them, "Why don't we get together and whoever goes in to talk contract first, call the other guys and tell them what they're talking about." That's as far as it got. Neither of them ever called.

The only guy I ever discussed contracts with was Bart Starr. He called me one time and said he was having contract problems, and asked if I would be willing to talk to him about it.

"Sure," I said. "What's the problem?"

"Well, they're talking about this kind of contract and this kind of money," whatever it was.

I told him exactly what I was making and how long my contract was for. "If you can use it to your advantage, more power to you," I said. If I was satisfied with what I was making, I can't help it if another guy makes more.

One year I played three-quarters of a season without a contract. I always figured I could work things out. We finally resolved it, and he [Carroll Rosenbloom] was supposed to defer money from my contract and invest it for me. I liked to defer money whenever possible and live off what I made in the off-season. I told Carroll, "You know where to put it. You have stockbrokers working for you."

He told me he would, but he never did it. Now he could have made up some story about it being against the rules or something like that, and I would have bought it, because I'm not the brightest person in the world when it comes to these things. However, he did give me interest on the money that I had, and it came to about $15,000 extra. Money wasn't a big thing with me. I just enjoyed playing.

On Quarterbacks

You see these guys with the real strong arms, and they're late with everything they throw. That's why they throw so hard. The whole thing is to throw the ball with rhythm, with timing, and according to the defensive man's position on your offensive man's position. If he's got him covered so that if you throw it high, it will be intercepted, then throw it low and make him go get it. Or you throw it short and make him come back for it. Or drop it over his head. They don't get that done anymore.

On Playing in San Diego at the End of His Career

The whole coaching staff there was incompetent. I asked a coach about two weeks before we were going to play a preseason game, "When are we going to put in the two-minute offense?"

He said, "What's that?"

I said, "You know, the two minutes before the half, the two minutes before the end of the game. We can win a lot of ball games there. Control the game, get on down and score."

"Oh, that," the coach said.

I waited for him to tell me what it would be, and finally he said, "Both backs flare wide, and everybody else hook inside; both backs flare inside, everybody turn out."

I was flabbergasted. "You don't really expect me to do that, do you?" I said. "Can I just put it in?"

He said OK, and I put in our two-minute offense. It was funny. I'd call a play in the huddle and the receivers would end up in the wrong place. It got to where I was hollering at these guys, and Deacon Jones, who was on the team, came to me to talk about it.

"You can't be hollering at the black brothers like that!" he yelled at me.

I got right up in his face and said, "I can't? That goes for you, too, you big son of a bitch." I finally got them to where they understood what I was trying to do. When I got to San Diego, I walked into the dressing room and pulled two or three of the receivers out of there and onto the field. I said to them, "If you expect me to throw to you, you can get your ass out here so I know where you're going."

Tommy Protho was the coach in San Diego my second year there, and all he wanted me to do was ride up and down the sidelines with him in his golf cart and listen to him tell me what kind of expert he was in bridge.

I was just out of place in San Diego. I saw stuff I had never seen before, marijuana and other things. We never had that in Baltimore. The worst thing we did was drink a beer. To see those people take pills and smoke grass instead of going out and having a beer after practice was strange for me. They used to sit up there and smoke marijuana coming out of a big volcano-like thing. I walked in one time to see this big block of wood sitting on the desk, with three rubber hoses sticking out of it.

"What the hell is that?" I asked.

"We're smoking some grass, man," one guy said.

"You guys gotta be some dumbasses," I said. "How do you expect to play football doing that? Or maybe you don't really play football out here." They had all the problem players in the league there at once. They used to smoke marijuana going to practice.

On Working with a Young Dan Fouts

I was working with Danny Fouts in his rookie year. Harland Svare, the Chargers head coach, had asked me to take the quarterbacks and help out with them. I put them through the same drills I had always done—setting up, quick cuts, and other stuff. I was trying to help Danny. They liked to use this Green Bay–type offense, with the flare back coming out.

I said to him, "You've got to put the ball down the field, 15 to 18 yards down the field. Forget those backs. We don't need those backs. If you get into trouble you can just drop it off to them if that is what you want to do."

It was the fourth week of training camp, and one of the coaches, Bob Schnelker, came over to me. He would holler and scream a lot, which drove me crazy. He said to me, "The coaching staff got together and had a meeting. We decided that we don't want you working with Fouts anymore."

I couldn't believe it. "We decided it was a conflict," said Schnelker.

I went to Danny and told him I got the orders not to talk to him anymore. He couldn't believe it either. "You've got 17 years of experience and they don't want you to talk to me anymore?" I told him they could tell me all they wanted to not to work with him, but we would work something out.

On Colts Coach Don Shula

Shula was an excellent coach. He was probably one of the best in the game. His best coaching was done in Miami, though, not Baltimore. He had players in Baltimore that didn't really need a lot of coaching, guys like Gino Marchetti and Raymond Berry and Jim Parker. But Shula was a hollering and screaming kind of guy. He loved to scream, and that drove me crazy. I really didn't pay a lot of attention to it. I just came out and did what I knew I could do with the game plan. I didn't pay much attention to what he was yelling.

On Working with Raymond Berry

Raymond would come in on a Tuesday. He'd take the films and watch them on Monday, and then come in on Tuesday and say, "Here's what I want to do. I want to run sidelines three different ways. I want to run the post this way and a quick out here. I want to run about five patterns on this guy. I know what I want to do there. You're going to have to control the rest of it. I can't tell you what to do or how to do that."

I'd say, "We'll work on these things this week, get our timing down, and then proceed to the game. Whether we run them from a 68 formation or a 72 formation or the wing formation is basically up to what I see out there."

That's what we did. He would come back to the huddle and say, "I've got this guy on a 15-yard sideline." He would run the pattern and we hit it.

On Leadership

There are a lot of ways to lead. You can lead by talking out, hollering and screaming, or you can lead by example. I led by example. I'm not a hollering and screaming kind of person. I don't have a lot of time for nonsense. If a guy wants to pull some shit on me, he's in the wrong huddle. We're here for business and this is what we are going to do. You go do your job, he'll do his, and I'll do mine. You can't win without that kind of cohesiveness. This is the way it's going to be done. If you don't like it, then put me on the bench.

On How He Became a Quarterback

When I was in high school (St. Justin's in Pittsburgh), my coach, Max Carey, put me in at quarterback. I was a halfback but our quarterback broke his ankle a week before the first game of the year. He said to me, "You're going to be my quarterback, so you better learn the plays." So I learned the plays in a week and went in the game and got my ass handed to me, 48–0 or something like that.

But the coach would keep saying to me, "You're the quarterback, you're the boss out there. You have a reason for everything you do. I don't care if you fall down or run a quarterback sneak, you'd better have a damn good reason for it." I would come out of a game and he would ask me why I did this or that, and I'd better have a damn good reason for it.

On His Greatest Fear as Quarterback

My greatest fear was that I was going to be typecast, predictable in what I was going to do. If I came out on a third down with six to go and ran a sweep every time, defenses are not dumb, and they will know it's coming. They've got their scouting and they'll see what my tendencies are. Whatever I

120

did one week, I would check on Monday or Tuesday to see where I might be getting into some kind of habit.

What I considered to be a compliment to me was something that I overheard from Henry Jordan. We were playing Green Bay in Baltimore, and we scored 13 points within a minute and a half to win the game. It was fourth down and time was nearly out. We were measuring for the first down, and I was standing on the line of scrimmage. I heard one player ask Henry, "What do you think he's going to do?"

Henry said, "Shit, I don't know. He does all sorts of funny things back there."

That was my main thing—never be predictable. Never let a defense dictate or say this is what he is going to do in a certain situation. You can't allow that to happen. You've got to be willing to put in the time and effort and study it.

On Joe Thomas, Bob Irsay, and His Last Days with the Baltimore Colts

Joe Thomas, the Colts general manager under owner Bob Irsay, was a jerk. I remember we had a meeting at the Super Bowl in Los Angeles when Washington was playing Miami. Joe Thomas said to me, "You can't throw anymore. You can't play anymore. You're not going to play another down in a Baltimore Colts uniform."

They fired head coach Don McCafferty, sat me on the bench, and made John Sandusky the interim coach. John came to me and said, "Look, I've got my orders."

I said, "I know, whatever you want me to do. But let me tell you one thing. Don't expect me to run out the clock for Marty

Domres [the new quarterback] or anyone else as far as that's concerned. I'm not going to do it."

Sandusky said he would never put me through that. Then one time we were playing in Baltimore against the Buffalo Bills that season. We were struggling, and then Domres got hurt. I had my jacket on, and I was sitting on the bench. I didn't say a word. Sandusky looked over at me, and I looked at him. His hands were tied, so I took my coat off, put my helmet on, and went on the field. About the same time there was an airplane flying over the field, pulling a banner that said, "Unitas We Stand." People in the stands were going crazy. The first play I handed off to Lydell Mitchell and he fumbled, but we recovered the ball. The next play I completed a pass to Eddie Hinton that he ran in for a touchdown. I came off the field to a standing ovation, looked up at where Joe Thomas was sitting, and gave him the finger.

We had another meeting at the end of the season, again at the Super Bowl, this one with Thomas, Irsay, my lawyer, and myself.

Irsay came in and said, "What's the problem with you guys? You can't get along?"

I said, "I don't have a problem. Thomas has the problem. He put me on the bench and told me I would never play another down in a Baltimore Colts uniform. He doesn't want me here."

"Suppose we trade you," Irsay asked.

"That's your privilege," I said. "I don't have any say in that. The only thing I would like is that if you're going to trade me, find out what teams are interested in having me, and then come back and tell me. Then I'll tell you what teams I would go to. Give me a choice of two or three clubs I might like to go to."

"OK, fine," Irsay said. "We'll get back to you."

Six weeks later, I got a call from a sportswriter at about 7:00 in the morning. He asked me, "What the hell are you doing going to San Diego?"

"What are you talking about?" I said. "I'm about to leave for Florida to speak to the Florida Quarterback Club."

"John, they traded you to San Diego for $150,000 just for the rights to talk to you and future considerations," the writer said.

About a half hour later, Ernie Accorsi [the Colts public relations man] called me and said, "John, Joe Thomas wants to talk to you."

"Fine, put him on," I said.

"No, no," Ernie said. "He just called me and asked me to call you to see if you would talk to him."

This was crazy. I couldn't believe how stupid this guy Thomas was. "Joe says he'll talk to you around 9:00 A.M.," Ernie said.

"That's too late," I said. "I'll be on a plane. Phone Joe, tell him to dial my number now, I'm here. I'll talk to him."

About 10 minutes later the phone rang. "John? Joe Thomas. Just wanted you to know we traded you to San Diego. Good luck." And then the line went dead.

That's when it really hit the fan. NFL commissioner Pete Rozelle called me because this whole thing turned into a big controversy. He asked me to come to New York, and I met with Rozelle, Irsay's lawyer, and Joe Thomas. Rozelle asked, "What's the problem?"

"There's no problem," I said. "These guys didn't live up to what they said they were going to do. They told me one lie after another." I told Rozelle about our meeting in Los Angeles and the agreement we had.

Irsay's lawyer said, "That was a misunderstanding. It was you who was supposed to find out who was interested in having you and then come back to us, and then we would make the deal."

"Mr. Rozelle," I said. "If I'm not mistaken, it says in our players agreement that nobody under contract in the NFL has the right to talk to any other team in the league. Isn't that right?"

"Yes," Rozelle said.

"Case closed," I said.

Rozelle asked the lawyer and Thomas to leave the meeting, and then, when it was just the two of us, said, "Now what do you want to do to settle your contract?"

"It's a $300,000 contract, 10 years at $30,000 with a job in the front office," I said. "I'll take $200,000 and you won't hear anything from me."

"That sounds fair," Rozelle said.

A week later, Rozelle called me. "They offered you $50,000," he said. Then he hung up.

On Playing with John Mackey

My first impression was, "Hey, we've got a tight end who can get deep. He has speed, and if his pass-catching ability is as good as his other attributes, we've got ourselves a winner."

To me, tight end is one of the most, if not *the* most, important positions on the team. He does two things—he makes your passing game go, and he makes your running game go because of his blocking ability. John could do that. He had great quickness. He had some problems sometimes catching the ball early on, but that would change with time. His blocking was superior.

I discovered I had to get the ball to him quick. As he's breaking, that ball has to be with his first step, because his strength was that once he had the ball, he was tough to bring down.

I saw him run against Detroit on a little play where it looked like the whole team got a shot at him. There was another play against the Chicago Bears on a little pop pass across the middle, and at least eight or nine guys hit him. But John just knocked them down and kept on going and got into the end zone. It was something like a 4-yard pass, but he turned it into a 65- or 70-yard touchdown. It was a great play. All I could do was stand back there and clap.

CHAPTER 8

TEAM BROTHER, UNION BROTHER

Although I was close to John Unitas, there were obviously experiences that we could not share. I was a black man entering a white man's business, and there were not many black men with the Colts that I could share those experiences with. One of the teammates who helped me when I came in as a rookie and who became a very close friend of mine was tackle Jim Parker. And then there were some players who weren't even teammates that I grew close to because they went into battle with me off the field. Brig Owens was one of the union brothers who put his career on the line, like so many union representatives did, to drag the NFL kicking and screaming into the 20th century. I spoke with both men in preparation for this book, and I wanted to share their insights.

JIM PARKER

I think Jim Parker was the greatest offensive lineman that has ever played in the NFL. Now, I may be biased, having played next to him. I loved playing next to Jim. He played every position along the line and was great at all of them. He was one of those guys who just punished you. He smothered you.

I'm not the only one who believes that Jim Parker was one of the greatest the NFL has ever seen. Jim was named to the top 100 NFL players of all time by *The Sporting News* and was inducted into the Pro Football Hall of Fame in 1973 along with teammate Raymond Berry.

For 11 seasons, No. 82 was the anchor of the offensive line that made our Baltimore Colts offense so successful. He spent the first six years at tackle and the next five playing guard, and he went to the Pro Bowl in both positions on a regular basis.

Jim wasn't a legend just in pro football. He was one of the all-time greats in college football as well, leading the Ohio State Buckeyes from 1954 to 1956. He started in Columbus as a defensive tackle on the 1954 national championship team. Coach Woody Hayes moved Jim to the offensive line playing guard the following year, and Hayes said that Parker "was the best offensive lineman I ever coached." During Parker's time at Ohio State, the Buckeyes won a national title and two Big Ten championships, and they had a record of 23–5. Jim won the Outland Trophy in 1956, the honor presented by the Football Writers Association to the best college lineman in the country. He was the first black man to receive the award. Jim was later named to the College Football Hall of Fame, and *Sports Illustrated* put him on their all-time college football team. He was the Colts' number one draft choice in 1957, but although

Hayes thought very highly of Jim as an offensive lineman, the reports are that he still told Baltimore coach Weeb Ewbank that in the pros, Jim would probably be better as a defensive lineman. That may have been true—we'll never know. But I can tell you I'm glad that Weeb and the Colts didn't listen, because I loved having him on the line with me on offense.

Jim had a bunch of nicknames on the team: Jumbo Jim, the den mother, mother hen, and the guardian, because he watched out for his teammates so well. But he particularly looked out for John Unitas. "It didn't take me long to learn the one big rule," Jim said. "Just keep 'em away from John. I remember coach Ewbank telling me my first summer in camp: 'You can be the most unpopular man on the team if the quarterback gets hurt.' How could I ever forget that?"

At 6'3" and between 270 and 280 pounds, Jim was still one of the fastest linemen in the league. He exploded off the line on running plays and plowed over everything in his way on the field. And he was even better at protecting his quarterback. He had quick feet and great balance, and his blocking technique allowed Unitas to become the great quarterback that he was. He was a role model for offensive linemen like Art Shell, Anthony Munoz, and others who followed him. They were great players, but Jim Parker did it first and did it the best.

Parker exemplified what made the Colts such a special team. He had a bad knee in 1967 that wasn't getting any better, so he voluntarily retired to make room for another player who could help us. "I can't help the team and I won't deprive 40 guys of their big chance," Jim said. At the time, we were undefeated. Coach Shula said, "It was one of the most unselfish moves ever made in sports. Jim has stepped aside strictly to help the team.

He will be remembered as one of the greatest offensive linemen in pro football history."

He is also one of the greatest friends I ever had, and one of the greatest men I have ever met. Here are some of his thoughts and recollections, in his own words, about Ohio State, the Colts, and playing with me.

On First Meeting John Mackey

I followed John throughout his career at Syracuse. He was there with Ernie Davis and came after Jim Brown, who was my roommate in New York when we were there for the All-American awards in college.

When the Colts drafted John, I knew the way they played at Syracuse and knew that John could help us. Their coach, Ben Schwartzwalder, insisted on coming off the ball and exploding to push their running game. Now when I first came to the Colts, we never had a running game. We always depended on Johnny Unitas' arm. But when John Mackey got to Baltimore in 1963, we were finally able to have a running game. We had good running backs, like Lenny Moore and Tom Matte, but until John came we never had what we called a postdrive block. We just fired straight into the guy and hoped like hell that the back could get five yards or slip through a crack and do the best he could.

I remember the first time John and I hooked up. He had a hot left, flank right, or whatever the hell it was. Anyway, John lined up on the left side. That meant we had a double team on the end. I didn't believe there was anyone else in the world who could come off the ball as fast as I could. That was one of my secrets. I could get into a guy real quick. John had a two-and-a-half-yard split. He came off the ball like a bullet and stood the guy straight up. All I had to do was blow him over. I said to myself, "Wow, that can't be." So we went back to the huddle and I asked Unitas to call the same play. He called it again, and John did the same thing. It was different because we could do it together naturally. Whoever got to the guy first was the post and the other guy was the drive. I thought it was the first time it was ever done that way.

This guy was quick and he could get off the ball. He was the quickest man for five or ten yards that I had ever seen. And when he caught the ball, watching him move down the field was extraordinary. He could run around defenders or go over them, and he could go all the way, get outside, and outrun them. I thought he was spectacular.

On Being Drafted by the Colts

They always sent Buddy Young to handle the black players, and they sent him to Ohio to talk to me. But I said I wasn't going to Baltimore. I was going to Winnipeg in the Canadian Football League. That was my first choice then. I had a friend named Kevin Jones who was from Steubenville. He was in California, but he played for Winnipeg. He called me and told me that he could get me $40,000 or $50,000 in Winnipeg because he was the only black living in the area. He said, "If you can brave the cold, you'll do all right." But then I decided on the NFL.

On Being a Rookie in 1957, and Comparisons to John Mackey

John reminded me of myself when I was a rookie, because when I first got to Baltimore, I didn't take any crap from any

131

veterans or let them treat me like a rookie, with all that stuff like, "Hey rookie, move the bags over here," and that kind of garbage. My attitude was that even though I was the fourth tackle, playing behind three people, when the season began the starting job would be mine. The veterans used to laugh at me when I said that. They would say, "No way, this guy has been here for five years." But I believed the job was going to be mine. I didn't want to play behind anyone. Now, it didn't start out that way. In my first exhibition game against the Chicago Bears, the Colts threw 47 passes. I wasn't used to that. We threw the ball more that day than we did in all my four years at Ohio State. In the first half I played against rookies and it wasn't so bad. Then in the second half they threw a very big and very powerful man against me: Doug Atkins, who was a legend in the NFL. Man, did he give me a lesson that day. Over the years Atkins and I had some fierce battles, but I think I got the better of them. I learned from those lessons and others during training camp, so by the time we left Philadelphia after the last exhibition game against the Eagles, I was the number one tackle.

After that I told the other tackles who were playing behind me, "You had better find somewhere else to play, because I'm never going to get hurt. I don't believe in anybody spelling me for relief or anything like that. This is my job."

That was the same feeling I had when John came. He was very impressive. We had what we called big dummies when we had to double-team blocks. And we had Raymond Berry, who was the out end on my side. When John came over on the strong side, I went back on the short side or the strong side of the field. It was different, and you could feel it. I would be laughing, because the guys on the other side, like Atkins or

Roger Brown from the Lions, they knew they had an ass-whupping coming, but they didn't know when it was coming. That's the way I felt: very confident. John came, and he felt the same way. He didn't wait for Unitas to make something happen. It was our responsibility to make something happen, and we could do that with a double-team block. It didn't matter who was throwing the pass then. We didn't have to wait on the arm for a pass to be completed. We just started right there at the line of scrimmage, kicking somebody in the butt and making things happen. That was the way we got things started.

On Encountering Racism with the Colts

There were a hell of a lot of places that were off-limits to us in those days. During training camp you couldn't even get a beer. We had to get our beer to go. We couldn't even go to the movies in Westminster [in Carroll County, Maryland, a rural county about 20 miles from Baltimore where the Colts trained at Western Maryland College]. We had this one black dude that we disguised as white. We took him down to the movie theater and we were told, "He can come in, but you all can't." We went back to our rooms and laughed all night. He went to the movies and came back and told us all about it. He was a big tackle. He didn't even realize that he might have been lynched or beaten up. They let him in, and he was black. I was from Georgia, so I was familiar with that kind of racism.

I told the black players what was going on when they came to the Colts. Colts owner Carroll Rosenbloom told us he would bring movies to camp for us. And then there was a time when we had a choice of moving camp to either Pittsburgh or Canada. But I didn't want to move. I wanted to stay. I didn't sleep in

Westminster one night in 11 years. I was out of there every night at 11:00 P.M. When the lights went out, I went out. I got caught twice in 11 years. We would sneak out the back door and head for the highway. I had a flat tire one night and it was raining, and this white dude got out of his car with a tire iron.

"What's the matter?" he asked.

"I just got a flat here," I answered.

"As long as I can see you, you can use my tools," he said.

So he loaned me his wrenches and equipment, but he kept his tire iron with him, watching me the whole time.

When I came to the Colts they had a seven-man black quota. They didn't give a damn about how good the eighth or ninth man was—if he was black, he didn't make it. One time we played in Texas, and they separated us from the white players. They stayed in a regular, decent hotel, and we stayed in a fleabag hotel with no air-conditioning, and it seemed like it was 130 degrees there. They separated us in Miami as well.

One time we were in New Orleans and needed to get back to the hotel before curfew or else coach Shula would fine us. But we couldn't get a cab to take us back. We got in one cab, and the driver yelled, "No, no, no, get away from here. I'm not going to let a black ride in this cab." And he took off and left us there. We were only four blocks from the hotel and probably could have walked back in time, or close to it, but we were angry then and didn't get back until about 3:00 in the morning. Shula had a note for me on my door that said, "Bring your asses to see me when you return." We went to see Shula and told him that we couldn't get a cab. But in the team meeting later that day, he announced that he was going to fine us. He later came to me and said, "I had to do that." But that made me angry. I didn't mind getting fined if I was wrong. But this time I was right.

Things started to change in the NFL when John Mackey and Willie Richardson and other blacks came into the league as well, and could do the job at different positions. They had us all playing the same positions before, but once we showed that we could do well at other positions, like John did, the seven-man quota seemed to vanish. We had John Mackey from Syracuse and Willie Richardson from Jackson State, and these players weren't wasted draft choices. They were superior ballplayers. They stayed for a long time and they weren't in and out of the lineup. I think Don Shula had a lot to do with it because he accepted us for what we could do. I remember one time during a game, Unitas threw a pass to John and the pass was wobbly. It got picked off and they went all the way for a touchdown. Unitas came off the field and said, "The offensive line penetrated too deep." Shula shot back, "Like hell it did. You just threw the ball like a lame-assed duck." And he jumped all over Unitas instead of the offensive line.

On Encountering Racism at Ohio State

Woody Hayes told me that he could only play three blacks at one time. I walked off the field and went back home to Toledo. They had to send someone to come bring me back. At the time, no blacks could live on campus in Columbus. It was Hayes' first year coaching there, and I wound up living with him. I knew for a fact that he wasn't a prejudiced man. But he had rules and regulations that he had to follow. The two daughters of Olympic athlete Jesse Owens came to Ohio State and they were living about two miles from campus. Then Jesse came to the school and met with the president of the college. Jesse told him, "My daughters are going to stay on campus." They were the first two black girls to live on campus.

On Playing Against Tommy Nobis

Tommy Nobis, the middle linebacker from Atlanta, was the toughest guy I ever faced. I played against all the great linebackers—Dick Butkus, Ray Nitschke, Lee Roy Jordan. Nobis wasn't very tall, but he had legs like tree trunks. He was a fireplug. One time we went to Atlanta and during a game, in the huddle, Unitas called my number to go against Nobis. I said to myself, "I'm gonna knock the hell out of this guy." I came off the ball and gave it everything I had. I hit him, and whoa, my neck went about four inches into my shoulders. I felt it all the way down to my toes. I thought I was dying. I went back to the huddle again and told Unitas, "Do it again, John, do it again. Call it again." So he called it again, and the same thing happened. Back in the huddle, Unitas asked me, "Want to run it again?" I said no, thank you very much.

On Playing for Colts Owner Carroll Rosenbloom

He was a typical owner. He played games with people. He would come in before a game and shake hands with everybody. With everybody he wanted to, that is. If he was mad at you, he would pass you by and not shake your hand. But that didn't really bother anybody. Carroll and Shula got into it because Carroll loved to parade through the locker room at the end of a game. Shula wouldn't let him in. Rosenbloom would bang on the door.

"Who is it?" Shula would yell.

"Carroll," Rosenbloom would yell back.

"Forget it. We're having a team meeting," Shula always shot back.

After one particular game when we got beat bad, Shula was in a bad mood, and Carroll wanted to bring about 15 people through the locker room. Shula yelled at him, "I run this team and if you don't like the way I run it, I'll be on the bus out of here. Nobody tells me what to do on the field or in my locker room."

Other than Shula, coaches never really had any authority under Rosenbloom. Shula was the one coach I played for who had authority over his own team.

Don McCafferty once asked me if I wanted a job as an offensive line coach. "What kind of authority will I have?" I asked. "Will I have the authority to pick my six tackles?"

"No, that's the head coach's job," he said. "They don't fire assistant coaches. They fire the head coach."

I said, "That makes sense. How much does the job pay?" They said that it paid $45,000 a year but that I would have to work year-round, with two weeks' vacation. McCafferty talked about a lot of other things, but my mind was made up when I walked into the meeting. I was just playing along with him. I thought to myself, "I could make that much money on the banquet circuit."

Then he said—and I knew this was Carroll Rosenbloom talking, even though he wasn't there—"Go up to the board and draw me a 4-3 defense." Now a 4-3 defense is a basic defense. It's like asking a 12-year-old to say his ABCs.

I said, "Don, will you do me a favor?"

"What?" McCafferty asked.

"Will you take this job and shove it up your ass? This is the first time I've ever been able to tell you what I really think." I already had a job, and it just felt good to tell him that. It felt so good because he was belittling me, telling me to draw a 4-3 defense. It had to be Carroll, because I really don't think McCafferty would have asked me to do that. After considering me to be the best offensive lineman in the league, he was going to ask me to draw a 4-3 defense?

On Meeting Colts Owner Bob Irsay

After I retired in 1967, I didn't go back to Memorial Stadium until after my election to the Hall of Fame in 1973. I was asked to come to the stadium to have my Hall of Fame ring presented to me. I was invited to be Irsay's guest in the owner's box. I walked out on the field and he walked up to me and grabbed me. He hugged me and started patting me on the back.

"Whattya say, Bub?" Irsay said.

"Who?" I answered back.

"Bub," he said again.

"Mr. Irsay, my name is Jim Parker, not Bubba," I said.

"I want you to have a good game, Bub," he said.

I told him again that I was Jim Parker and that I was there to get my Hall of Fame ring. They expected me to ride up with him on the elevator to the box. But I was thinking to myself, "I'm not getting in any elevator with this drunk. He might keep pushing the wrong buttons and we'll never get there."

"I'll meet you up there," I said to him. "I'll walk up."

I got up to the owner's box, and I sat down next to him. During the game I watched him at one point pick up the phone and yell, "Take that son of a bitch out! Take him out now!" And sure enough, the player came out of the game.

I sat there looking at this crazy man, thinking to myself, "I would pay $1,000 to see this lamebrain pick up a phone and call Don Shula and tell him to take somebody out of the game." Shula would have gone up to the box and kicked his ass.

I left at halftime. I couldn't take any more of it. They gave me my ring at halftime and I said, "Bye-bye."

On Having Big Daddy Lipscomb as a Teammate

One time Big Daddy lost his wallet when we were playing the Redskins. He had $600 in it. We had a valuables kit he could have put his money into, but he didn't. I didn't know he had $600. Anyway, we had just won a really tough game. Big Daddy was crying in front of his locker like a baby. Carroll came into the locker room after the game and saw Big Daddy blubbering. Big Daddy blamed Sam Sternoff, this locker room guy we had who could hardly walk due to his bad leg. He was in the shower, too scared to come out. Big Daddy was ready to break his other leg.

Carroll asked him, "What's wrong?"

"I had $600 in my wallet and that son of a bitch over there went and lost it," Big Daddy said, sobbing.

Carroll gave the money to Big Daddy right then and there. "Now let me see you smile, Big Daddy." And Big Daddy gave him a big grin.

On the Early Days of the Union

The front office pretended that they loved the union and they were all for the players. But we had lost a lot of money before John Mackey took over. Commissioner Bert Bell took all the bubble gum card money and the Coca-Cola endorsement money. He took everything for the commissioner's office. We never even heard about it. It wasn't much money, but he took it and we didn't find out about it until he announced it at the annual commissioner's meeting. Then, in 1959, we formed a union. Each of us paid $50. And things changed when John took over the union. Management had pretended they wanted to see progress, but then when they saw they couldn't control us anymore, they came out and started fighting John openly. You could feel the chill. Some of the players were scared to be part of it. They would stand in the middle of the road. We had to dicker for dues at the end of the year.

On the *Sports Illustrated* Controversy

Sports Illustrated was up in Baltimore one day, writing a story and comparing me with John Hannah, the lineman from New England. I said, "If I had been white, I would have made millions." I was All-Pro for nine years and played the Pro Bowl all those years as well. I was the best in the league.

So they asked me, "How do you feel about Hannah? Who do you think is the best?"

I said, "I'm the best offensive lineman who ever played the game. I'll let my record speak for itself. I'm in two Halls of Fame." I was just tootin' my own horn. But it got blown all out of proportion.

Now, I had tickets to the Colts games that had been set aside for me by Carroll. After the story appeared I went to pick up my tickets, and the lady at the box office said, "Carroll says you don't have tickets anymore." Carroll pulled my four end zone tickets. The Colts were playing the Oilers that day, and when the owner of the Oilers heard what happened, he gave me four tickets on the 50-yard line. Later I asked Carroll why he pulled the tickets. It hadn't even occurred to me it was about the *Sports Illustrated* story.

Carroll said, "I didn't like what you said in *Sports Illustrated*."

"You could have picked up the phone and talked to me about that," I said. "You didn't have to backstab me for the four damn tickets." And after that, I never went to another Baltimore Colts game again.

On Leaving the Game

I hurt myself in Philadelphia and ended up sitting in the locker room for a half hour. Nobody came to see me about my leg. I couldn't even get my stuff off, so I cut it off. I got a cab and went all the way back to Baltimore. I paid the driver $100. They had been looking for me all over Philadelphia. Shula called the house and asked, "Where the hell were you? You're going to be fined. Why didn't you wait for the doctor?"

I said, "I waited for a half hour."

I played in 139 consecutive games. I had never been hurt. And I stepped in a hole and messed up my knee. That was the end of my career.

BRIG OWENS

Brig Owens played 12 seasons in the NFL as a defensive back, from 1966 to 1977. He played his entire career with the Washington Redskins and was one of the leaders of the 1972 Redskins NFC championship squad that went to the Super Bowl.

He is second on the all-time list of Redskins in interceptions, with 36, and first in yards on interception returns, with 686.

What drew Brig and me together, though, was the union. He was a man who wanted more for himself, his family, his teammates, and his union fellowship, and he devoted himself to that work not only as a player representative during the time I served as president, but also later on, filling the role of assistant executive director and associate counsel to the union from 1979 to 1984. During that time, Brig helped develop the Players Association's financial planning, career counseling, employee assistance, and substance abuse programs.

He also got a law degree and is now a partner in Bennett & Owens, a sports management and real estate development firm in Washington.

Brig had the good fortune to play for a coach who recognized the value of having men who were natural leaders—often player representatives—on his team. Unlike many coaches, George Allen did not see player representatives as a threat. He saw them as a resource.

"I played at a time when if a person was a player rep, they were either blackballed or traded," Brig said in an interview for the book *The Washington Redskins: An Authorized History*.

"Well, we had about seven or eight player reps on our team at one point," he said. "George would pick them up because they were leaders. With all those leaders on the team, he didn't have to do a whole lot to get players to perform. He enjoyed having leaders around him."

Though I loved Shula and respected him as a truly great coach, one of the greatest of all time, if I couldn't have played for Shula, I would have loved to have played for George Allen. It would have been fun to play with Brig, too, instead of against him, since our bond off the field within the union was a strong one.

Times have changed and so has the relationship between owners and players, at least to some extent. But Brig's recollections, shared here in his own words, illustrate the trials and tribulations that he and I and others went through.

On First Encountering John Mackey

I was the assistant player representative in 1967 and Pat Richter got traded, so I became the representative. It was something that at the time I really wasn't crazy about. The philosophy of the Redskins then was that they always wanted to have a younger player as an assistant player representative so that he could learn as time went on.

I remember John becoming president of the union, but what I always remember about John was that he was the most feared tight end in the business. There are no John Mackeys in the game today. He was the complete tight end. Not only could he run with the ball, but he was a great blocker and a mean tight end. He was mean. John could have a down block and he could take the entire side on his own. That would open up a lot of space for the running back. I can remember getting ready to play against the Colts and watching so much film of John Mackey, I knew what he ate.

One of my teammates, Lonnie Sanders, told me, "Brig, when John catches the ball, be careful about coming up on him to tackle him because he likes to straight-arm with his fist." Now, I'm thinking to myself, "If he doesn't catch it, I don't have to worry about tackling him, or his straight arm. But if he does catch it, I'm gonna let him know I'm there."

I was young and cocky. John was phenomenal. He would run through people. I developed techniques. I worked out angles at which to approach big men like John.

On Facing Fellow Union Representatives on the Field

I think there is a competitive spirit among athletes that, even if you are friends, when you compete against each other, you're going to make sure you are at your best. It's not unlike situations in the real world. You come up against a person in a business transaction, and you negotiate and you want to do the very best you can. It's the same thing in sports. You want to do the best you can.

On the Costs of Working for the Union

It was very difficult in those years to be a player representative. If a player became one, he was almost sure to be traded, or the talk would start that he had lost a half step or something like that, and then he would be benched. It happened to John. Here was a man who was selected tight end of the decade, but because of his union activities, they sat him down. Then he couldn't get into the Hall of Fame.

On Race and the Union

Management used to try to separate white and black players based on leadership. . . . I remember one time we came into a bargaining meeting, and all of the chairs were brown. Joe Robbie, the Miami Dolphins owner, was a member of the management council. He walked in, and the majority of the players there were black. Robbie said, "Hmmm, the chairs are the same color as the guys on the other side." What kind of racist comment was that?

On the Challenge of Keeping the Membership Happy

A professional athlete is used to having results within short periods of time. If he is playing football, he has to be successful in four downs. Within 60 minutes of play, he's got to know whether he's a success or a failure. In baseball you might have four pitches to decide. In basketball it's up and down the court, the shot clock, the whole bit.

So athletes deal with success and failure within a short, defined span of time, and they believe that you can get the same kind of results in the real world. It doesn't happen that way. So coming back to the players and trying to explain to them what went on at a meeting, and why you can't get certain things done in a collective bargaining agreement, becomes an ordeal. They don't understand that the easiest thing for management to do is sit back, say no, and let the players put the pressure on themselves.

The players sometimes don't understand that if they expect to have a strong union or a strong association, then they as a group have to be strong. They have to show the other side that they are strong. You can have the best negotiator in the world and the best public relations firm, but they're just the quarterback—you can have the best quarterback in the world, but if he doesn't have a front line, forget it.

On the Superstar Athlete

The superstar athlete makes more money, and superstars always have the feeling that management is going to take care of them. They figure, "If I don't get too involved, management is going to take care of me and I'm going to work for the club." It isn't until they have one foot out the door that they realize they need help. Or they are out the door and come back and

145

ask the union for help. "I didn't know what was happening. I didn't realize they would do this to me. I didn't realize they would try to question my integrity in terms of what my injuries are. I didn't realize they would cut off my insurance." They cut off insurance one year when guys had wives who were pregnant. A lot of players didn't realize that owners would do those sorts of things. The superstar players believed they didn't need to support the union.

On John Mackey as President of the National Football League Players Association

When John became president of the association, he was the person who really got us operating as a business. Prior to that, it was sort of like getting everybody together at somebody's house. John had a business background, and he said we had to have an office, an executive director, and secretaries. He said, "We have to have a place to represent the players where a guy can call in, a place where they can visit. We have to operate as a business so that we can get a certain amount of respect."

That was the true start of the National Football League Players Association. We went out and interviewed people. That's where Ed Garvey came from, as a result of John Mackey and the screening that we did.

CHAPTER 9

SUPER BOWLS WON AND LOST

By 1967, after four years, and particularly coming off my best season, I had become one of the leaders on the team. I had become a presence in the city as well, appearing on local radio and television shows and being active in the community. I had grown close to community leaders such as Dr. Ralph Jones from Morgan State, a man who was very influential in my life and grew to be one of my closest friends.

In most ways, I had been accepted in Baltimore and by my teammates. But there was still a very different way of life for the black man and the black ballplayer, no matter how much you believed you were accepted. In Baltimore everyone lived in segregated areas. Our black players lived in the inner city and the white players lived out in the suburbs—just like the population in urban communities everywhere across America in the sixties. It was the age of the "white flight" to the suburbs. Even the coaches lived out in the suburbs.

Another difference became apparent when I would go to the team offices downtown. I would walk in, Unitas and Matte might be there, too, and Shula would see us. He would say to Unitas something like, "How are you doing? How's Dorothy [Unitas' wife]? How are the kids?" Then he would turn to Matte and ask, "How's Judy [Matte's wife]?" Then he would turn to me and say something like, "How's your weight?" That really bothered me, and I had an opportunity to tell him that.

"Why is it that it's Judy and Dorothy with those guys, but with me it's, 'How's your weight?'" I asked Shula. "You don't know my kids? The difference is that when it comes time to cut someone, I'm only No. 88, but if it's Tom, you have to talk to Judy, the kids, and everyone."

To Shula's credit, he learned from every experience. After we talked he got to know Sylvia. He had us up to his house for dinner. And when Dick Szymanski got married and none of the black players showed up for the wedding and the reception, Shula called me at home and asked, "Why aren't you here?"

"We don't have a baby-sitter," I said.

"Take the baby to my house and then come on out," he said.

So we took the baby to Shula's house and then went to the reception and had a great time. Later we went back to Shula's house. He had made a point of getting to know Sylvia and the kids and learned from what I said.

Race may have segregated the Baltimore Colts, but it didn't divide us. We stood together as teammates in times when it counted, on and off the field. One time after an exhibition game in Atlanta, and only five minutes before curfew, everybody wanted to run out and grab something to eat. We went over to a restaurant across the street from the hotel. Freddy Miller, who had gone to Louisiana State University, and Bob Vogel from Ohio State were sitting at the counter, and a few other guys were eating as well, when Willie Richardson and I came in. The restaurant workers told us that they couldn't serve us. After that, everybody from the team ordered double and triple orders to go, and then, just as they were about to get the food, everyone just got up and left without the food or paying for it. The guys said, "If you can't feed them, you can't feed us."

If race was not dividing the Baltimore Colts, it was certainly dividing the country by 1967, and of course, during the riots of 1968—Baltimore was no different. It put me in a difficult position because when Baltimore was on the verge of going up in flames, city officials turned to people like me, Lenny Moore, and other black Colts to try to calm things down. That's one of the ways I became a leader beyond the black community—when they were afraid that the city was going to be destroyed. I wasn't a leader when they decided to build decent, affordable housing on the other side of town. They didn't call me then and say, "We know you're one of the leaders. We want you to get in on this."

The mayor of Baltimore at the time was Tommy D'Alessandro. I got a call from his office asking me to come down to the National Guard Armory to help them calm things down. I turned to Sylvia and said, "The mayor wants me to come down there."

"Well, I guess you should go," she said.

"I don't know what he wants me to do," I said.

"He's going to want you to try to calm the city down," she replied.

"I don't know how to do that," I said. "I'm a football player."

"Evidently they think you can do something," Sylvia said. "Why don't you go down there and see what they want."

So I got in the car with my brother Elijah and we drove through the streets, while the National Guard was out in full force. Some of the guardsmen were from other states, so they did not recognize me when they pulled us over. We were ordered out of the car with bayonets at our back, and they searched us. At the same time the Baltimore police chief drove by, got out of his car, and yelled at them, "You've got the wrong guys!"

Then the chief turned to me and said, "I'm sorry about that. Mayor D'Alessandro asked me to come and escort you to the armory."

I was steaming. "Hell, no, we're going home!" I yelled at the chief of police. "I don't need this. I almost got shot out here trying to help the mayor."

So I went home, and they called me back up, asking where I was. I told them that I would just as soon stay at home. It was disheartening to be called on that way. Why do some people think that because you score touchdowns or dunk a basketball that you are qualified to lead others? The guy on the corner burning things down has more to say. They ought to have talked to him.

After the riots I got involved in Camp Concern. It was a program we set up so that kids could leave the inner city and go to camp. I did that out of my heart. I didn't do it because I thought somebody was going to make me a leader or because I felt I was a leader. I did it because it was something I *could* do. I called

Governor Spiro Agnew and asked him for the money, and he told me how to go about getting it, which I did. I went to Hubert Humphrey to get more money for the camps. My position gave me access to people like Agnew and Humphrey. My position was an All-Pro tight end on the Baltimore Colts, and I tried to remember that my work on the field had to be successful for the work off the field to be successful.

It seemed like 1967 was the year that it would all come together. We had gotten so close over the last few years but came up short each time. We opened the season with the determination that we wouldn't let the season end early for us again. We had a rocky opener defensively, narrowly beating Atlanta 38–31 at home, but we settled down after that to pull off a string of decisive wins. We beat the Eagles 38–6 in Philadelphia, then pummeled the 49ers at home, 41–7, followed by a 24–3 win over the Bears in Chicago. Then we ran into a rough spot and the season seemed like it could have gone either way. We played the Rams to a 24–24 tie at home, and did it again the following week with a 20–20 tie against the Vikings in Minnesota. Despite two ties, we still hadn't lost a game, giving us a record of 4–0–2, and we went on another winning spree—seven straight victories. We won 17–13 over the Redskins in Washington; 13–10 over the Packers at home; 49–7 over the Falcons in Atlanta; 41–7 over the Lions at home; 26–9 over the 49ers in San Francisco; 23–17 over the Cowboys at home; and 30–10 over the Saints at home. We were undefeated, with an 11–0–2 record, going into the season finale against the Rams in Los Angeles, a team that had a 10–1–2 record. The Rams blew us away, 34–10, and we finished the season with matching 11–1–2 records, which should have set up a playoff. But there were no dates available for a playoff. The Falcons and the Saints had entered the league as expansion teams that year, so the conferences were divided into four divisions. The Colts, Rams, Falcons, and 49ers were in the Coastal Division. Because of the additional division playoffs, no time was available for a special playoff game to settle the tie between us and the Rams. The officials decided that the team who scored the most points in the head-to-head matchups would move on to the playoffs and the other 11–1–2 team would stay home. Since we tied the first game 24–24, the Rams' 34–10 win in the second game gave them the nod. It left us with little to show for what had been a remarkable season, what should have been a championship season. Our defense had set a club record, allowing the fewest number of points over a season—198—and Unitas completed 255 of 436 passes for 3,428 yards and 20 touchdowns. I continued to improve my numbers, finishing second behind Willie Richardson, who emerged as the leading receiver with 63 catches for 860 yards. I pulled in 55 catches for 686 yards, a 12.5 yard-per-catch average, and three touchdowns. As a team, we gained a total of 5,008 yards for an average of 357.7 per game. We had seven Pro Bowl players—Unitas, Vogel, Richardson, Fred Miller, Ordell Braase, Rick Volk, and me. But we didn't have a championship ring, and, by the start of training camp in 1968, we were convinced that we were a championship team.

But disaster struck first. On September 7, 1968, in an exhibition game against the Dallas Cowboys, Unitas suffered a severe injury to his right elbow while trying to avoid a rush. He tried to get the ball off by throwing a sidearm pass, but he was hit hard and wound up tearing the muscles in his arm. It turned out that the worst part of the injury wouldn't appear until nearly 30 years later. The muscles healed, but Unitas knew nothing of the undiagnosed nerve damage. In the last few years of his life, the nerve damage had such a terrible effect that he couldn't button his shirt or hold a pen with the same right hand that had thrown all those touchdown passes to me. The "Golden Arm" was nearly paralyzed when he passed away.

Without Unitas, how could we possibly win? We used to put all our faith in him. If we were down 10 points with two minutes to go, we figured he would win it for us. Thanks to Shula, though, we had a backup plan, and his name was Earl Morrall. Shula had traded for Morrall, a veteran NFL quarterback, in a deal with the New York Giants. Although he was no Unitas, Morrall had the experience to run an offense, and with a team like us behind him for the first time, Morrall showed he could be a winning NFL quarterback.

We opened up at home with a 27–10 win over the 49ers, and then went on the road for two straight wins, 28–20 over Atlanta and 41–7 over Pittsburgh. We were rolling with a 28–7 win at home over Chicago and a second victory over the 49ers, 42–14, this time in San Francisco. We were 5–0 and looked pretty unbeatable with Morrall at quarterback. We got a wake-up call from our old friends the Browns, who had Leroy Kelly at running back. They beat us at home, 30–20, to bring us back to earth—or so I thought. By the end of the season we had forgotten that lesson.

We bounced back to beat the Rams at home, 27–10, and continued on another winning streak—26–0 over the Giants in New York; 27–10 over the Lions in Detroit; 27–0 over the

Cardinals at home; 21–9 over the Vikings at home; 44–0 over the Falcons at home; 16–3 over the Packers in Green Bay; and 28–24 over the Rams in Los Angeles to end the season.

The Baltimore Colts finished the season with a 13–1 record without Johnny Unitas, something that would have seemed impossible before the season began. We had a devastating defense, and we didn't seem to lose a step offensively. We scored 402 points over a 14-game season and held our opponents to just 144 points. Morrall had a remarkable season, completing 182 out of 317 passes for 2,909 yards and 26 touchdowns. He performed so well that he was named the league's Most Valuable Player. And the change didn't appear to make much of a difference to me, at least on paper. I was Earl's favorite receiver, leading the team with 45 catches for 644 yards and five touchdowns. Willie Richardson finished behind me with 37 catches for 698 yards and eight touchdowns, followed by Jimmy Orr with 29 receptions for 743 yards—an impressive 25.6 yard-per-catch average—and six touchdowns. I also carried the ball 10 times on end runs and other plays for 103 yards, including a 33-yard run.

Though Earl liked to throw to me, and I caught 45 passes, it was a very tough year for me on the field. I had a rhythm with Unitas that I had developed from practicing so often with him. I would take a step and John would get me the ball, and always get it to me on time. He would tell me, "If I don't hit you quick on the pop pass, go behind the linebacker and I'll hit you in the next lane." By the way he threw the ball, I always knew if I was open, if I was in trouble, or if I had to knock it down. If I was wide open, he would put the ball out there and say, "Go get it." If I was in trouble, it was close-in to the stomach, and I would

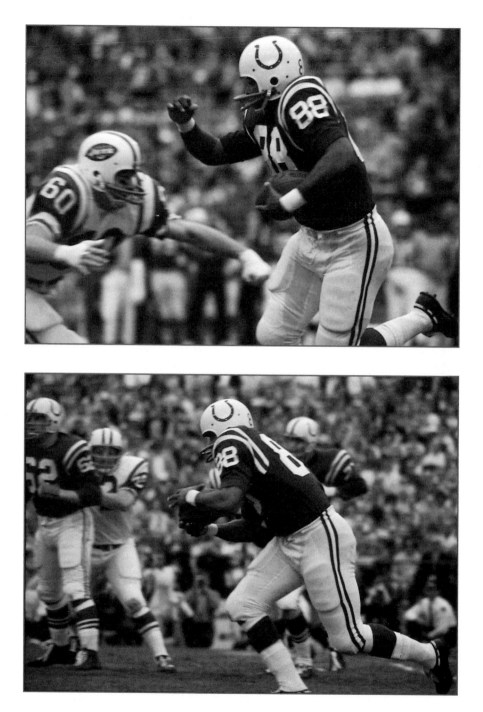

I caught three passes in Super Bowl III, but for a disappointing total of only 35 yards. We didn't get downfield very often during that game. *Photos courtesy of Vernon J. Biever.*

It looks like I'm smiling here in an interview with NBC's Kyle Rote after our Super Bowl loss to the Jets; perhaps it was just to keep from crying over the embarrassment of the loss. We went into Super Bowl III as 17-point favorites; maybe I was smiling because of how ridiculous that notion seemed after the game. *Photo courtesy of Vernon J. Biever.*

Trying to lead the union and the NFL from the stone age to the modern age of labor was a team effort. Here I'm talking to two quarterbacks, Fran Tarkenton and Roman Gabriel, during our brief strike in 1970. *Photo courtesy of AP/Wide World Photos.*

One of the benefits of being an NFL star and president of the NFL Players Association was the chance to meet famous and important people who accomplished so much more than we did on the football field. Here I'm with the astronauts from the Apollo 12 lunar mission (from left): Richard Gordon, Alan Bean, and Charles "Pete" Conrad. *Photo courtesy of AP/Wide World Photos.*

With Congressman and former NFL quarterback Jack Kemp at a black-tie affair. *Photo courtesy of the Mackey family.*

One of the biggest fights of my life away from the field was the lawsuit I filed against the NFL concerning their so-called Rozelle Rule (named after commissioner Pete Rozelle), which allowed the commissioner to control free agency. Here I'm standing outside a federal courthouse with center Bill Curry (center), who was the president of the Players Association in 1975, and Ed Garvey, the executive director whom I had brought into the union. The lawsuit paved the way for the free agency that players now enjoy in the NFL. *Photo courtesy of AP/Wide World Photos.*

I wasn't exactly "Superfly," but I was considered somewhat of a fashion plate while I played, and was once photographed for a fashion layout. I was no Frenchy Fuqua—I didn't have high-heeled shoes with fish swimming around in them—but I wasn't shy about looking good. *Photo courtesy of the Mackey family.*

This was my office during most of my career: Memorial Stadium, once called "the world's largest outdoor insane asylum" by one sportswriter because of the rabid passion of Baltimore Colts fans. Memorial Stadium is now gone, replaced by a new stadium that houses the Baltimore Ravens. The atmosphere that flourished at Memorial Stadium is something that will never be captured again. *Photo courtesy of the* Baltimore Sun.

Once during a press conference I was asked how I would respond to referees who might have a problem with my physical style of playing. I kiddingly showed that my reaction would be something like "I can't hear you." This was a special moment for me because it was the day I was presented with the Ernie Davis Award—which benefits the Leukemia Society of America—for not only my play on the field but also my charitable work. Ernie Davis, who the award was named for, was my teammate, roommate, friend, and brother at Syracuse University before his tragic death. *Photo courtesy of AP/Wide World Photos.*

When I was finally elected to the Pro Football Hall of Fame, the normal procedure at the time was for inductees to be presented with their rings during halftime ceremonies at the home field of the team they had played for. But the Baltimore Colts no longer existed, having left town in 1984 to relocate in Indianapolis. I wanted nothing to do with the Indianapolis Colts, so I arranged to have my ring presented to me during an exhibition game in Baltimore in 1992 with the Miami Dolphins playing and my favorite coach, Don Shula, making the presentation. At that time no NFL football had been played in Baltimore for eight years. *Photo courtesy of the Mackey family.*

My family, all grown up, at my Hall of Fame induction (from left): my daughter Lisa and her husband, Butch, with their son, Benjamin; my daughter Laura; my wife, Sylvia; and my son, Kevin, his wife, Sandra, and their daughter, Vanessa. *Photo courtesy of the Mackey family.*

My Hall of Fame bust. *Photo courtesy of the Mackey family.*

catch it knowing I was going to get hit. But when Earl was playing quarterback and I released inside, he pumped. When he pumped, I hesitated because that was when he should have thrown the ball. I would say to myself, "I'll go over to the next lane." So I did, and he lobbed it. When he did that, I figured I was wide open. Well, one time against the Vikings, safety Karl Kassulke gave me a bone-crushing hit because I wasn't used to reading Morrall. I lay on the ground. Everything hurt. The trainer came out and asked me, "Where does it hurt?" I said my feet, my head, my ears, everything. Then I heard Shula say, "Get up, Mackey. They can't hurt you." And I got up. It was like a reflex. Hell no, they couldn't hurt me. Of course, I couldn't walk on Monday.

That wouldn't have happened with Unitas because I knew what to expect. I had his cadence drilled into me. Jim Mutscheller taught me in my very first year that the most important thing was to get off on the count. I had Unitas' cadence down so right that when he said, "Hut," I was moving, and on "One," I was sticking. When I got in there with Morrall, I could never play like that. I always had to wait for his count, and it messed me up. It just seemed that Earl always caught me on the wrong leg. When he was pumping, he should have been throwing because I was always on the other leg. If I'm on the left leg when the linebacker is coming, I can catch it, but I can't protect myself from the clothesline. If I'm on my right leg, I can catch it and throw out a stiff arm. With Morrall I was never on the right leg.

Still, if you are a professional, you learn to make adjustments. I adjusted, we all adjusted, and it seemed like we adjusted very well. We were an impressive team on paper—

maybe one of the best of all time. At least that's what our press clippings were saying. And if they weren't saying it, I, like a fool, was. "This is the greatest football team ever," I told reporters. "I'll tell you why. We have a great defense, a good offense, and spectacular special teams, plus a terrific place kicker and a fine punter. The great teams have had one or more of those things, but rarely all five together. Then there is the togetherness on our club. We're in great shape." Man, I wish I could have taken those words back.

We did nothing to dispel that notion in the playoffs, beating Minnesota 24–14 on a cold, rainy day to win the Western Championship. We went into the half with a 7–0 lead and then opened the game up in the third quarter, when I caught a 49-yard touchdown pass from Morrall and Mike Curtis returned a fumble 60 yards for another score, giving us a 21–0 lead. After the Vikings scored on a short pass from Joe Kapp to Billy Martin, we answered back with a 33-yard field goal by Lou Michaels. Minnesota added a final, late score on a seven-yard pass from Kapp to Bill Brown. Morrall had completed 13 of 22 passes for 280 yards, and I caught 3 of those passes for 92 yards.

After the game, Kapp only added to the hype by declaring that the Colts were the finest football team he'd ever seen. Then we put the finishing touches on the hype by rolling over the Browns, our longtime nemesis, 34–0. We held the Browns and their great running back, Leroy Kelly, to just 56 yards rushing and a total of 173 yards of offense. Then it was on to the new big game in the NFL, the Super Bowl.

The Super Bowl was part of the merger agreement three years earlier between the NFL and the American Football League. The two leagues agreed to set up a game between the two champions. The Packers were NFL champs in 1966 and 1967 and blew away the AFL champions, the Kansas City Chiefs and the Oakland Raiders. The NFL players looked on the AFL teams with contempt—many sportswriters and other observers felt that way as well. At various times before the game, we were 16- to 17-point favorites over our opponents, the New York Jets. No one gave the Jets a chance to win— except the Jets, and it turned out they were the only ones that counted.

There were all kinds of melodramas playing out before the game took place in Miami. First there was the return of Weeb Ewbank, the former Colts coach, who was then coaching the Jets. A few former Colts players on the Jets roster were looking for payback, particularly Johnny Sample, who was more than willing to engage in trash talking. And the talk heated up, particularly when our place-kicker, Lou Michaels, nearly got into a fight with Jets quarterback Joe Namath in a Fort Lauderdale bar. Then Namath made the now infamous declaration that he "guaranteed" a victory. That seemed like a ridiculous statement, but it turned out the Jets had the right frame of mind going into the game and we didn't. They had learned from watching films that we were not the superteam that everyone, including me, made us out to be. They were confident in their ability to score on us, and that confidence came from being prepared—not from the press clippings that we put too much stock in.

As everyone knows, on January 12, 1969, before a crowd of 75,389 at the Orange Bowl in Miami, the Jets handled us with ease, shocking the entire sports world by scoring 16 points and holding us to zero until the fourth quarter. When we did finally score, making the final tally 16–7, it raised all sorts of questions about whether or not Shula had made a miscalculation at quarterback. Morrall had led us through a great year, but Unitas was healthy and ready to play in the Super Bowl. Nothing had changed our belief that with Unitas at quarterback, we always had a chance to win. So the question was, should Shula go with Unitas or Morrall in such a big game? He went with Morrall, and we'll never know what might have happened if Unitas had gotten the start. The only score we had in the game was after Unitas came in.

I caught three passes for 35 yards, but one of them could have changed the entire game early. On our first play, Morrall threw it to me. I had it all planned out—I was going to run that ball in for six points. I had been thinking about it and envisioning it ever since Shula announced that they were going to hit me on a diagonal flick play to get me one-on-one against the linebacker, Larry Grantham. The ball came to me, I caught it, and I started to run. And do you know how Grantham tackled me? By the shoelace! I fell down. There was no way it would have happened if I had run my natural pattern and not pressed so hard to do what I had thought about doing. I got a first down, but I should have gone all the way. Then there was the play that everyone talked about when it was all over. It was late in the first half, and we had the ball on the Jets 41. It was second down, with nine yards for a first down. Morrall handed the ball to Tom Matte, who tossed it back to Morrall— a flea flicker. Jimmy Orr was wide open in the end zone, but Morrall couldn't see him and wound up trying to get the ball to Jerry Hill. Jets safety Jim Hudson intercepted the pass.

When it was all over, Namath had completed 17 of 28 passes for 206 yards while Morrall struggled, completing 6 of 17 passes for 71 yards and three interceptions, all coming in the first half. They rushed for 142 yards, with 121 by one of my hometown guys from Long Island, Matt Snell, for a total of 337 yards in offense. Matte ran the ball well, gaining 116 yards on just 11 carries, but we made too many mistakes. Even Unitas, who went 11 for 24 for 110 yards, had one interception. We went into the game way overconfident, and when we realized we had a tough game on our hands, we panicked because we couldn't believe we were losing to an AFL club. After that we couldn't get anything going. The lesson is that if you keep your feet on the ground you have a better chance of winning.

We had one more game to play, but none of us felt like making the trip to the Pro Bowl. It was my fourth straight Pro Bowl and the fifth in my then six-year career. We had eight Pro Bowl players—Bob Vogel, Willie Richardson, Earl Morrall, Tom Matte, Fred Miller, Mike Curtis, Bob Boyd, and me—but no Super Bowl ring. It was galling to have to show up at the game and face our NFL counterparts having been the first to lose to an AFL team.

When training camp opened in the summer of 1969, we were still hung over from the Super Bowl loss. In fact, we never really recovered that season, and things were out of sorts right from the start. Running backs Terry Cole and Jerry Hill were hurt during camp, and the old story about using me at running back resurfaced. Strangely, after six seasons at tight end, they were still enamored with using me in the backfield. Shula told reporters, "I've talked to John about the switch and he was very unselfish about making the move." But I got hurt after two days, and that was the end of yet another running back experiment. That knee injury never seemed to heal that year, and the slightest bump made it swell up. I wound up missing two games and was never quite right during the season. The season began as a disaster, as we lost our first game 27–20 to the Rams at home, and then were embarrassed, 52–14, by the Vikings in Minnesota. (They went on to win the NFL title but suffered the same indignity that we did in the Super Bowl— losing to an AFL team, this time the Kansas City Chiefs.) We bounced back to win our next three games: 21–14 over the Falcons in Atlanta; 24–20 over the Eagles at home; and 30–10 over the Saints in New Orleans. In our next three home games we lost to the 49ers, 24–21, but defeated the Redskins, 41–17, and the Packers, 14–6. But it was up and down all season, back and forth. We lost to the 49ers 20–17 in San Francisco; beat the Bears 24–21 in Chicago; beat the Falcons at home 13–6; tied the Lions at home 17–17; lost to the Cowboys 27–10 in Dallas; and then finished with a 13–7 win over the Rams in Los Angeles. We finished the season with an 8–5–1 record— certainly not good enough to get into the playoffs. Unitas had his worst year ever with the Colts, completing 178 of 327 passes for 2,342 yards, 12 touchdowns, and an embarrassing 20 interceptions. When Morrall played, he completed 46 of 99 passes for five touchdowns and seven interceptions. Willie Richardson and Tom Matte tied for receptions, with 43, and I had 34 catches for 443 yards—my lowest total since 1964. It was also the worst year Shula had as coach of the Baltimore Colts, and it turned out to be his last. He left to join the enemy, going to the AFL to coach the Miami Dolphins. There were a lot of other changes going on: Don Klosterman replaced Harry Hulmes as general manager and three Colts—Ordell Braase, Dick Szymanski, and Bob Boyd—retired.

Because of the merger agreement between the NFL and the AFL, that year three NFL franchises moved to what had been the AFL. That name—the American Football League—was done away with. It became the American Football Conference (AFC), and the former NFL was renamed the National Football Conference (NFC). The three teams that moved to the AFC received $3 million and joined the Denver Broncos, Buffalo Bills, Miami Dolphins, Kansas City Chiefs, Oakland Raiders, San Diego Chargers, Houston Oilers, Cincinnati Bengals, Boston Patriots, and New York Jets in the conference. Those three teams were the Cleveland Browns, the Pittsburgh Steelers—and the Baltimore Colts! It seemed as if we were being banished. It seemed as if things were changing too fast, as if everything fell apart because of that loss in Miami. The Colts would be playing in a strange conference, and the only coach I ever had in the NFL had left. His replacement was a good man who was very different from Shula—the easygoing Don McCafferty. (He was nicknamed Easy Rider because of his personality.)

Things were still out of sorts throughout the preseason. My knee was still bothering me, and we seemed like a lost team when we opened the season at home against San Diego. We struggled but won, 16–14, on a last-minute field goal by our rookie kicker, Jim O'Brien. Little did we know, that was an omen.

The next week we played the Kansas City Chiefs, the NFL champions, coming off their 23–7 upset win over the Vikings in Super Bowl IV. We were overwhelmed, 44–24, in our first appearance on *Monday Night Football*. We had lost our identity as winners, and we weren't sure if we would ever get it back. But we got healthy again, thanks to our new conference and the fat wins that came with it. We went on the road for three straight weeks and beat the Boston Patriots 14–6; the Houston Oilers 24–20; and the New York Jets, in a small measure of revenge, 29–22. When we came back to Baltimore, we were a surprising 4–1, and we treated our hometown fans to two big wins, a 27–3 beating of Boston and a 35–0 shutout of the Miami Dolphins and their new coach—Don Shula. We went back on the road to beat the Packers, a once-great franchise that had fallen on hard times, 13–10. The Baltimore Colts were 7–1 and all seemed right with the world. We weren't particularly pretty or as dominating as we had been before, but we were winning, and that was the bottom line. We nearly lost the next week to Buffalo at home, but managed a 17–17 tie. Then Shula got his payback in our second game against the Dolphins, who won 34–17 in Miami. But that was just a misstep. We got back on the winning track in a close game the next week, a 21–20 win over Chicago at home. Then we beat Philadelphia at home, 29–10, followed by a 20–14 win over the Bills in Buffalo and a 35–20 season finale victory over the Jets.

Remarkably, we finished the season with a record of 11–2–1. It was especially remarkable given some of the statistics we compiled that year. We outscored opponents 321 to 234, but Unitas had a poor season, completing 166 of 321 passes for 2,213 yards, only 14 touchdowns, and 18 interceptions. Morrall completed 51 of 93 passes for 792 yards, nine touchdowns, and four interceptions. Eddie Hinton led the team in receptions with 47 for 733 yards and five touchdowns. My numbers were down again, just 28 catches for 435 yards and three touchdowns. Our leading rusher was Norm Bulaich, and he ran for just 426 yards on 139 carries, an average of 3.1 yards per carry. We had just three players named to the Pro Bowl, and none of them were on offense—defensive end Bubba Smith, middle linebacker Mike Curtis, and safety Jerry Logan.

Yet we went into the playoffs feeling confident that we had a chance to make up for what had happened two years before. In fact, it was our mission. We shut out the Cincinnati Bengals 17–0 before a hometown crowd that could also sense we had a shot at redemption. The following week, in the AFC championship, we faced the Oakland Raiders at home. They came into the game very cocky, still rubbing the Jets and the AFL win in Super Bowl III in our face. But we established ourselves early. Jim O'Brien kicked a 16-yard field goal to give us a 3–0 lead in the first quarter. We made it 10–0 in the second quarter when Unitas hit Hinton with a long pass and Bulaich went over from the 2-yard line. We appeared to have the game in hand when Oakland quarterback Daryle Lamonica got nailed by Bubba Smith and had to leave the game with a thigh injury before the end of the first half. That wasn't good news, though, because it meant that 43-year-old George Blanda came in the game. Blanda had only added to his legendary career that season by becoming a successful relief quarterback for the Raiders, either kicking last-minute field goals or coming in to throw touchdowns to pull out victories. First he kicked a 48-yard field goal before the half to cut our lead to 10–3. Then, in the third quarter, Blanda hit Fred Biletnikoff for a 38-yard touchdown pass, and the score went to 10–10. Before we went back on the field, Unitas turned to me and said, "Enough of this shit." You could see in his eyes that there was no way he was going to let us lose that game. He moved us down the field and put us in position for O'Brien to kick a 23-yard field goal. On our next possession, we scored again on an 11-yard run by Bulaich to take a 20–10 lead. Early in the fourth quarter Blanda came back to lead an 80-yard scoring drive, capping it off with a 15-yard touchdown pass to Warren Wells to cut our lead to 20–17. It appeared that Blanda would work his magic again when he got the ball back and began another drive, but this time the defense stopped him twice with interceptions by Jerry Logan and Rick Volk, and Unitas finished the Raiders off by hitting a 68-yard touchdown pass to Ray Perkins for a 27–17 victory.

Just like that, we rode Easy Rider all the way back to the Super Bowl, although we found ourselves in the strange position of representing the old AFL—now the AFC—against the NFC champion Dallas Cowboys, in the same place where we were embarrassed two years before: the Orange Bowl in Miami. It had a totally different atmosphere this time. We weren't as up and down emotionally between the intense practices on the field and relaxing away from it. We had a calm confidence in our preparation. We had better control of the hype, and our practices were about workouts and previews. We felt like we were ready for anything that Sunday as more than 80,000 people filled the stadium.

So what happened? We played like a semipro team, giving up three interceptions and four fumbles. Fortunately, the Cowboys were worse.

Ron Gardin went back to return a punt and fumbled, so the Cowboys got the ball on our 9-yard line. They couldn't get the ball into the end zone, though, and Mike Clark was forced to kick a 14-yard field goal to give Dallas a 3–0 lead. They added another Clark field goal in the second quarter, a 30-yarder, to take a 6–0 lead. Then came my redemption.

Unitas called a 15-yard route to Eddie Hinton down a seam on the weak side in the Dallas defense. My job as tight end on the right side of the line was to make sure nobody came on the blind side and hit Unitas when he went back, and then clear out the deep area. The ball was snapped, I checked and then went downfield. I went about 22 yards and was about 6 or 7 yards behind Hinton when I looked back inside. The ball was there in front of me, as big as could be, ready to be grabbed, and I was there to grab it. Then I turned and headed for the end zone, and before I knew what happened, I had gone 75 yards for a touchdown. Hinton had tipped the ball, and so had defender Mel Renfro, which made it a free ball for either the defense or offense, according to the rules at the time, although Dallas defenders argued that they never touched the ball. As the ball was in the air, either Charlie Waters or I was going to get it. I had the better position and pulled it in, scoring what was then the longest touchdown in Super Bowl history.

We should have taken the lead, but Jim O'Brien's extra point attempt was blocked, so it was a 6–6 tie game. The next time we got the ball, Unitas wasn't able to find a receiver and he pulled the ball down to run with it. But he fumbled after being tackled by Lee Roy Jordan, and the Cowboys recovered on the Baltimore 28-yard line. Several plays later, Dallas took a 13–6 lead before halftime on a seven-yard touchdown pass from Craig Morton to Duane Thomas.

The Cowboys kicked off to start the second half, and it happened again. Jim Duncan fumbled and Dallas recovered. The Cowboys ran Duane Thomas into the line and appeared to nearly score, when the ball came loose and Duncan, of course, given the bizarre nature of the way this game was going, recovered, although the Cowboys claimed otherwise. One of our tackles, Billy Ray Smith, kept yelling, "It's our ball, it's our ball." On our next series, though, Unitas was intercepted, took a brutal hit from George Andrie, and had to leave the game. Now we had to rely on Earl Morrall again to get us through this title game. He moved us down the field to the Dallas goal line on a 26-yard pass to Hinton and 21 yards to Roy Jefferson, but Norm Bulaich failed to get into the end zone on three carries, and then Morrall missed on a fourth-down pass.

No matter. In this game, a second chance was always a fumble or interception away. Duane Thomas fumbled again in Dallas territory in the fourth quarter. McCafferty wanted to go for the score, so he called the flea flicker—the same call from Super Bowl III in which Morrall failed to spot Jimmy Orr in the end zone. Morrall came out and pitched the ball to Sam Havrilak going right, and Havrilak was supposed to throw it back, but he couldn't because the Dallas linebackers had penetrated too deep. Meanwhile, Hinton was downfield and all alone at the Cowboys' 20, and Havrilak found him. Hinton seemed on his way to a touchdown when a Cowboys defender stripped him of the ball. It bounced and rolled nearly all the way through the end zone, but at the last second a Cowboys defender got the ball, and Dallas had possession. We were crushed yet again by the flea flicker.

We were down 13–6 midway through the fourth quarter when Rick Volk intercepted a Morton pass at the Dallas 33 and returned it to the Dallas 3-yard line. Tom Nowatzke took it over for the score, and the game was tied 13–13. It looked as if the game was going to go into overtime. Dallas got the ball on their own 25 with less than two minutes left in the game and began a drive down the field. But linebacker Mike Curtis intercepted another Morton pass and returned it to the Cowboys' 28. We were going crazy on the sideline while McCafferty was trying to calm us down. Two plays later, with nine seconds on the clock, Earl Morrall turned to Jim O'Brien in the huddle. O'Brien was a junior in college when we lost to the Jets, and before he attempted his field goal, Morrall wanted the rookie to know what this meant to all of us. "There's no wind, and there's no way these guys up front are going to let anybody in," Morrall said. "I'm going to give you the best spot you ever had in your life. You just kick that thing straight through."

Everything seemed to happen in slow motion after that. The Cowboys were yelling all kinds of things at O'Brien. "They were trying to distract me," O'Brien told reporters. "Then, for a second, I remembered our practices and how Billy Ray Smith would holler at me. I said to myself, 'This is only Billy Ray yelling.' I knew I was either going to win or lose the game for us."

The ball was snapped, Morrall put it down, and O'Brien nailed it, right through the middle of the uprights. I didn't know whether to laugh or cry, so I just started jumping up and down and screaming at the top of my lungs. Dallas took the kickoff, and then the final play of the game was, appropriately, a Morton pass that was intercepted by Jerry Logan. The

Baltimore Colts and I were the winners of Super Bowl V and world champions. When all was said and done, the Blooper Bowl had 11 turnovers, but only one set of numbers counted—the ones on the scoreboard that had us with 16 points and Dallas with 13 points. After the game, I joked with reporters about the circumstances surrounding my catch. "The ball was hit two or three times before I caught it," I said. "It got to me while I was on a dead run so then I did my 9.1 to the end zone." I was smiling at them when I made the 9.1 reference. After all, that was the world record for the 100-yard dash.

After all the battles I had fought on the field, I had finally won the big one. No matter what else happened to me, I would always be a Super Bowl champion. That would be important to me because the battles off the field—battles with the powers that ran the NFL—were much more difficult and dangerous.

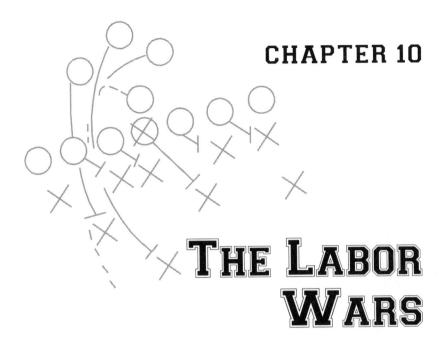

CHAPTER 10

THE LABOR WARS

For most of my playing career, I had total tunnel vision. All I wanted to do was play football and be the very best I could be. Away from the field, I was interested in business. After all, I had gone to Syracuse wanting to be a lawyer. During the off-season, I worked to develop a career away from the game, doing media work and other enterprises. I remember Ordell Braase had his locker next to mine and would sometimes ask me if I knew one thing or another, and usually I wasn't aware of what he was talking about. He would say to me, "You've got to look at more than just being a football player. You've got to look at pension plans and this and that." But when it came to football and the locker room, I was focused on making sure I could make the catch or the block when I needed to.

Then Bob Vogel, who came in with me as a rookie in 1963, became our player representative to the NFL Players Association. He was a very articulate guy and would always take the time to explain everything. That was when I really got interested in what was happening on the business side of football. I got more and more interested, but little did I know that my interest had reached the ears of the powers of the league, or at least the front office of the Baltimore Colts. Carroll Rosenbloom and his associate Sig Hyman began lobbying me to run for president of the Players Association. I had no idea I was being set up as a pawn in their plan to control the association. Eventually that plan would backfire big-time. During my tenure as Players Association president, owners would use a lot of words to describe me, but *pawn* wouldn't be one of them.

Sig said he was going to show me how to be a successful businessman. Pretty soon we were doing a lot of things together. I'd go over to his house and play tennis, and our families would socialize. Then one day, while Sylvia and I were at his house, Sig suggested to me that I should run for president of the Players Association.

"What do I care about the Players Association?" I answered.

"You ought to think about it," Sig said.

I didn't really think about it very much, but before I knew it, Sig called me and said, "I've got 10 votes for you. You don't have to get many more. If you can't go in and get elected president, you aren't trying."

This was in January 1970. At the time, Buffalo Bills quarterback Jack Kemp was president of the AFL Players Association. John Gordy had resigned as president of the NFL

Players Association, and I was the candidate to replace him. Kemp agreed to give me all of his votes for president after the two associations merged. So there I was, president of the entire Players Association. At the same time, I had recently undergone surgery for knee trouble. It was tough, but I had responsibilities to meet, and I did the best that I could, telling reporters shortly after I was elected that in negotiations with the owners, we would seek increased pension contributions; the reworking of the option clause in a player's contract (at the time, NFL bylaws allowed a player choosing not to sign a contract with his team to play an option year with a 10 percent cut in pay, after which he would be a free agent, a price too steep for players to pay); a larger share of revenue from product licensing; and improvements in preseason and severance pay.

Soon I would go to my first big meeting with Alan Miller, a former football player who became a lawyer and then was chosen as counsel for the AFL Players Association and the new association after the merger. The meeting was in Hawaii, and I found myself sitting in a big suite across from NFL commissioner Pete Rozelle, Cowboys boss Tex Schramm, and other owners. When I walked in the door the first voice I heard was the big baritone of Schramm.

"I always wanted you to play on my team," he bellowed. "I've been after you since high school."

They were stroking me from the minute I walked in the door. Others, like Ralph Wilson from Buffalo and Rankin Smith from Atlanta, were there as well, all singing my praises and slapping me on the back. Before I left, Schramm gave me some advice. "Let's keep it in the family," he said. "No outside lawyers, and nothing to the press." I left the room thinking to myself, "This is nothing, man. We'll get together, negotiate, and sign a contract, and that will be that."

The party was over quickly when we met again, this time in New York. This wasn't in some hotel suite. We met in a big boardroom at the league headquarters, sitting at a huge table with 26 chairs—a real stage for power plays. Sitting across from me were Rozelle, Schramm, a group of owners, and a heavyweight in labor relations, their lawyer, Theodore Kheel.

I didn't know who Kheel was, and I didn't know why this guy should be here. He wasn't part of the "family" that Schramm was talking about, at least I didn't think so. I picked up quickly that this meeting was going to be very different from the first one.

"Who's he?" I asked, pointing to Kheel.

"Ted Kheel, our labor counsel," Schramm said.

"What do you mean, labor counsel?" I answered back. I was sitting over there with just Alan Miller and they had 10 guys on their side. I thought, "I'm not going to let anything happen here until I get more players in here, because you don't play football 10 on 1."

Kheel handed me a piece of paper and said in an imperious tone, "Young man, as a precondition for recognizing you as the bargaining agent, I demand that you sign this."

I picked it up and started reading it. Alan Miller grabbed it out of my hand, read it, and told me to sign it.

"I haven't read it," I said.

"I've read it, and it's OK," Miller said. "It's boilerplate."

From that moment on, I had problems with Alan Miller. I looked him in the eye and said, "No, I can't sign this until I've read it all. For instance, it says here that I must sign away the rights to negotiate preseason pay in perpetuity, and that sounds like a very long time to me. I'm not going to sign anything that has that in it."

It may have been just about preseason pay, but there was a power play going on in that room that I didn't like. They had told me in Hawaii that there would be no outside lawyers, but here I had Kheel trying to intimidate me.

"You're going to have to sign it before we go any further," Schramm said.

But I wasn't going to sign that paper, not then, under those circumstances. "I'm going to go outside and talk to my lawyer," I said.

Kheel replied sarcastically, "It's called a caucus."

I looked at him hard and really wanted to punch him. I told Miller that I had no intention of signing the paper. "Are you telling me that my great-grandchildren would have to play under the same terms I am playing for?" I said to him. "In perpetuity?" I turned around, walked out of the room, crumpled up the document, and stuffed it in my pocket. Then I went into Rozelle's office and called a labor professor named Norman Feinsinger at the University of Wisconsin. I had read his name in a newspaper article in Baltimore. "Professor Feinsinger?" I said. "My name is John Mackey of the Baltimore Colts. I'm president of the National Football League Players Association and I'd like to talk to you."

"Where are you?" he asked.

"I'm in New York at Pete Rozelle's office," I said.

"Leave right now and go to a public phone," he told me.

I left the building and found a public phone. I called him back, and he told me to get on a plane and come talk to him, so

I flew to Wisconsin and met with Professor Feinsinger. I showed him the crumpled piece of paper.

"The best thing you did was not signing this," he said. "They would have shoved it down your throat. It's illegal. You couldn't sign it because you can't sign away the rights of unborn children in perpetuity, which is what that means. You need some labor counsel." He recommended Leonard Lindquist in Minneapolis, a senior partner in the firm of Lindquist and Vennum. I hired him, and he was a terrific counselor. He leveled the playing field between me and the owners. But after a while, I felt that I needed something different from our labor counsel.

"Leonard, you've got to get me a young lawyer, one that I can argue and fight with," I said. "I can't fight with you. I was raised to respect my elders and betters, and you're too good for me."

Leonard, to his credit, understood, and later he introduced me to a young lawyer named Ed Garvey who would go to work for us. That's when the Players Association came of age. Up to that point, the union had been considered a necessary evil by both players and owners. It really had little power or collective bargaining rights, so negotiations usually just dealt with such issues as preseason play, pension plan contributions, or similar items.

We had another meeting, in Bimini, an island in the Bahamas, and it got pretty ugly. Actually, it was on Rozelle's boat. I flew down on a little airline called, of all things, Mackey Airlines. When I got to Miami, I met Alan Miller and Sig Hyman, who was in charge of our pension plan, and we chartered a small plane to Bimini, where we boarded Rozelle's boat. We didn't talk contract, but there was a lot of drinking going on. They were pouring a lot of Jack Daniels into my glass and acting like my friends, telling me that I could fly down and use the boat anytime I wanted to. But I didn't fit into that scene. I wasn't one of them. I wasn't a drinker, and I didn't smoke. And if I wasn't drinking, I figured I could stay alert and work over Schramm for information, which I did. They were pouring me drinks, and I was quietly pouring them out on the carpet or anyplace I could find in the corner where I was sitting.

It smelled terrible in that spot the next morning, and Schramm started screaming at me. "You're not an honorable man," he yelled. "I'm going to take you out and feed you to the sharks!" Somehow they found out that I had poured the drinks out. Schramm was mad because I had violated his good-old-boy rule of "one man drinks, every man drinks," and the captain of the boat, Captain Otto, was mad because I messed up his carpet.

It got very strange and very ugly in there. Captain Otto practically threw my breakfast at me, so I took the offensive and changed the mood of the room. "If you ever throw anything at me again, I'm going to break your neck," I said to Captain Otto. "Now take this garbage away and make me a proper breakfast before you are fed to the sharks."

Then I went after Schramm. "You're going to throw me over?" I yelled. "I'll throw you over." The atmosphere changed after that. It was clear that this was not a party and that I was mad. They were apologetic, and I think it was on the boat that they finally realized they were not dealing with a mere pawn in this game of chess. And if they didn't know it then, they certainly knew it when the Players Association went out on strike over pension and other benefit issues in the summer of 1970. The owners clearly did not realize that this was a different time for the union. They figured we would just buckle and sign what they wanted. But we didn't, and that's why I led the players in a walkout right before the start of the exhibition football season. The owners and I had met for six months and talked and talked and nothing happened. Five days of talks with federal mediators did little to resolve the dispute. Then the owners locked out the players. When they lifted the lockout, we went on strike, on July 30. We were seeking $26 million in pension payments over four years, and the owners were offering $18 million total for that same period. The strike sent the owners scrambling to find a way to deal with the problem, and some of the ways they tried were pretty bizarre.

One time I was at Duke Ziebert's restaurant in Washington with my teammate and union confidant, Bill Curry. We were having dinner with Sargent Shriver, the former head of the Peace Corps, who was running for president. He was trying to talk me into backing him and getting the Players Association to work for Democratic candidates. In walked Washington Redskins owner Edward Bennett Williams, the famed trial lawyer, who treated Ziebert's like a second home. He saw me and yelled, "It's your fault!"

At the time, I didn't know who he was. "What do you mean, it's my fault?" I shot back.

"The problem we're having with the players and the owners is your fault!" Williams said.

I turned to Shriver and said, "Sargent, I don't even know this man. I don't mind taking criticism, but I'd like to know where it's coming from."

Shriver said, "John, meet Edward Bennett Williams."

I had heard so much about him that I asked for his autograph. Williams left to have dinner, but later that night he saw Shriver at the bar and asked if I would talk to him. I went out to the bar, sat down, and listened to one of the greatest minds in the history of the American legal system tell me about his greatest desire, which had nothing to do with a courtroom.

"You know, there's only one thing in life that I've ever wanted, and now that I have it, nothing means anything," Williams said.

"What are you talking about?" I asked.

"I always wanted to be in business with Vince Lombardi," he said. "And now that we're in business together, he's dying." And with that, Williams started to cry.

"You're killing him," Williams said between tears. "You've got to sign the contract for the players."

I couldn't believe what I was hearing. Then I found myself crying along with him. I could see why Edward Bennett Williams was such a great lawyer in court. We ended up sending Lombardi, who was in the hospital dying of cancer, a floral display for his room with a card that said, "Our sincere best wishes and prayers are with you. You are a great coach and a great individual to all of us." We meant it, too.

It was a cold, calculated tactic by the owners to use Lombardi as leverage in the labor dispute. But this was the full-court press. A few days later Rosenbloom called me and gave me the hard sell as well. Then I went to New York for a meeting with Rozelle, and the meeting consisted of riding around all of New York in his limousine. I asked him why we were driving around.

"The reporters are following us," he said.

"There are no reporters following us, Pete," I said.

We ended up in Philadelphia at Ed Sabol's house. We went out to the pool, where Rozelle said he wanted to talk about the contract. They showed the last page of the deal they wanted and told me to sign it. Then the telephone rang and someone called Pete to the phone. When he came back, there were tears in his eyes.

"Vince is dying," he said. "You know what that means? If he dies before you sign the contract, the public is going to believe that you killed him. You've got to sign it because he is the Kennedy of football. If you don't sign it before he dies, everything's going to stop, and we're going to lose the whole season."

I still couldn't believe what I was hearing. And it got worse. I had another session with Rozelle at his apartment. We were going to watch the College All-Star Game. Of course Schramm was there, along with Wayne Valley and Rankin Smith.

"You know the only friends you have in the NFL are in this room," Rozelle said.

I was thinking, "Man, if these are my friends, I know I'm in trouble."

"Do you really want to go down in history as the guy who killed the goose that laid the golden egg?" Smith asked. "We've all got it pretty good in this league, and with what you're trying to do now, you're going to ruin it. You've got to sign."

Of course, one side had it significantly better than the other. All I was trying to do was bring the deal closer to what Smith had claimed—for *all* of us to have it pretty good. But the pressure was hard and heavy to cave in.

We finally reached an agreement in a 22-hour marathon session on August 1. It was a four-year deal, worth $19.1 million in pensions and other benefits, an $11 million increase based on the 1969 levels, and for the first time players obtained disability, maternity, dental, and widow's benefits. It was a lifetime of lessons learned in labor negotiations. Even when I thought we had a deal, we didn't. It took another year before the agreement was finally signed, and they had to be forced into signing what they had already agreed to. The National Labor Relations Board ruled that the owners had an obligation to sign the agreement they reached with us following the brief strike in 1970. They were supposed to sign it at their March 1971 meeting, but they changed it and then signed it. We filed an unfair labor practice suit, and the owners had to finally meet their obligation. It was a grueling time that took its toll on my home life and my time on the field, and afterward I became convinced that active players should never negotiate for the union. No player should have to go through what I went through or be put in that position.

I tried to get involved in football again. I went to camp for the 1970 season, but the calls kept coming in for union business. As the season went on, it became painfully obvious that I was never going to be just a football player again.

The fight would continue. I filed a lawsuit in 1973 seeking free agency, an action that turned out to be a landmark decision in the field of sports law. Some reporters have referred to me as the football version of Curt Flood, the baseball player whose courageous efforts to fight the system for free agency paved the way for others to reap the rewards. My lawsuit was specifically against the so-called Rozelle Rule, which required a team that signed a free agent to give "fair and equitable" compensation to the team that lost the player. I contended that the rule stifled competition by limiting the bargaining power of players. No teams were willing to pay the price to sign free agents. It rendered free agency meaningless. The courts agreed with me, both on the lower federal level and the appeals court, determining that the Rozelle Rule violated federal antitrust laws. However, it didn't immediately translate into changes within the NFL. The courts said that the union and the owners had to bargain over implementation of the ruling, but the Players Association's subsequent labor agreements were unable to secure true free agency. It wasn't accomplished until the association found a different way to go at the problem—by decertifying itself and having individuals file lawsuits, which led to the 1992 decision by Minnesota judge David Doty that forced the league to agree to the form of free agency that exists today.

Even after I left the game I was still very much involved with the boardroom battles. I served as a player's agent for a while, working for the William Morris agency and representing players such as the Dallas Cowboys great Ed "Too Tall" Jones. I also would advise the association from time to time, when asked. In 1987—another strike year for the players—I delivered this speech at a players conference:

> I played pro ball for years and all of the games are
> still in my blood. I still remember that when the
> players were entering or leaving the stadium on
> game day, the fans would ask, "Hey, who is that?"
> And I still remember the vendors calling, "You

can't tell the players without a program." We could hear them, and in the stadium, on the field, in jerseys with our numbers, we knew who we were. We were athletes. Pros. We wore jerseys with our numbers to tell everyone who we were. And we knew why we were there. We were there to win. On the field, all of us knew. We knew that we had a special gift, that we had been blessed with special talents that allowed us to perform athletic feats that thrilled millions. We all knew that we had discovered these gifts when we were 10 or 11 years old. We all had trained and honed our bodies, running miles in the heat of the summer, lifting weights until we ached, doing calisthenics by the hour, driving ourselves to be the best we could be. We would and did go to any length to achieve our goal, and that "true grit" was, more than anything, what made us winners.

We all knew that our scholarships to college depended on our determination. Our abilities brought hundreds of thousands of dollars for our universities. We brought alumni and their gifts to our campuses and, in later years, television revenues. We all knew that we were working our way through college, and, by the reputations we won, we might make it to the pros. Back in college, that seemed like the ticket to financial success.

Many of us had to forsake in-depth education in college because of the demands of our sports programs and our coaches. But that was OK. We all thought that maybe, just maybe, if we kept working as hard as we had since we were 11 or 12, we could make it to the promised land of professional sports. The most gifted, the most tenacious, and the luckiest of us signed a contract. We became professional football players. We practiced long, bone-crunching hours five days a week. We played before millions of fans Monday night, Friday night, or Sunday afternoon, giving all that we had while trying to guard ourselves against serious injury. Many of us made television appearances to hype the game. We raised millions of dollars for charity, and most of us worked to better our communities.

But off the field came the haunting question—"Hey, who is that guy?" And the singsong of the vendors—"You can't tell the players without a program."

And the constantly haunting thought—how long will I be in the program? An average of five years—that was all. And then what? Who and what would I be after the game?

The owners knew who they were. They were behind desks making huge profits from the game. Between 1978 and 1982, football owners, many of whom declared they were just breaking even, were earning $5 million to $6 million per year per club. The press knew who they were. They were sitting at typewriters hyping the game. Neither the owners nor the press were out there getting bruised. They weren't getting injured, and they were not the stars. Nobody asked them to make the televised appeals for charity because the charitable organizations didn't think they had the appeal.

But despite all we did on the field, despite all we did for others, who were we? And more importantly, who would we be five short years after college graduation, when we were no longer in the NFL programs? We were athletes. We were entertainers. We were still the "go for the glory" guys of our college days. But we were men now, men with families, men with financial responsibilities. Who the hell were we besides No. 81?

I saw some of my teammates become businessmen while they were still playing. But then what if you woke up one morning and found out you had been traded, which is just a nicer word than sold? That weakness gave all of us a very weird feeling of who we were—or who we were not. We can never say for certain we are members of such and such a team and live in such and such a city. We can't even claim normal rights of American citizenship to choose where we work and live, or to join another outfit if the one we work for sends us to another town, does not let us use our potential, or doesn't pay us enough. We are only who we are until an owner tells us we are someone else. And that's why 20 years ago, we, the players, decided that we had to begin to determine for ourselves who we were, and, once we knew that, what we wanted. Then once we knew that, how to get what we wanted.

It didn't happen all at one time. It has been a slow process, stretching over many years. Until the end of the 1956 season, NFL players had not a single group benefit. There was no hospitalization program, no injury clause in the contract, and only two clubs paid their players for preseason games. None of the players liked it, but no one could do anything about it because each player acted alone. Then, in 1956, a small group of players representing 11 of the then 12 teams requested a meeting with the late Bert Bell, then commissioner of the NFL, concerning a pension plan and insurance benefits that would provide players a degree of financial security later in life. This action of unison was the first step in the formation of the NFL Players Association. This was the first step in our awareness of who we were as players, what we wanted, and how to get it.

In January 1957, Kyle Rote and Norm Van Brocklin, along with legal counsel Creighton Miller, presented specific proposals to Commissioner Bell. Among these were recognition of the association by the owners; minimum salaries of $5,000; expense money for preseason games; inclusion of an injury clause in the players' contracts; and shorter training periods. Though the association was not recognized by the owners, most of the proposals were accepted. With this victory, the association began to press for others. However, until 1968, the association did not engage in any kind of collective bargaining. Once a year, at the owners' annual meeting, the players were invited to a morning session and asked if they had any problems. They all gathered around a table—owner, player, owner, player—and very little was said or done until the players themselves began to set goals.

The basic goals were to establish certain economic benefits, a formal procedure for redress of grievance, and a contract that would govern the rights and obligations of both players and owners. And as they faced negotiations with the owners, the players realized that to be successful, they had two options: either they could become part of an outside labor organization that was knowledgeable in the process of collective bargaining but would bring, in addition to this asset, certain liabilities; or they could do the job of negotiating for themselves.

The reason was pressing. After the emergence of the Super Bowls in 1967 and 1968 and the merger of the NFL and the American Football League in 1968, interest in football skyrocketed.

The money skyrocketed as well, and the demands of the players to participate in the benefits of the game became more intense. However, their demands, such as increased preseason pay, were turned down.

Disappointed, the players considered joining an established labor union to increase their power in their relationship with the owners. But they decided to remain independent. In 1970, the NFL and AFL Players Associations merged to become stronger. This was the birth of the NFLPA as we know it today. I was fortunate to be selected as the first president of this new association.

It was obvious that the owners felt threatened by the power of the new, combined Players Association. During my first year as president, the owners no longer even recognized our new association as a legitimate bargaining organization. Only through our recognition by the National Labor Relations Board were we able to force the owners to the bargaining table. So you see, it was actually the owners who finally recognized who and what we were as professional athletes. We were labor. The owners had stripped some of the last romantic illusions from our childhood dreams of life as a professional athlete in the NFLPA. We fought and fought hard for revisions in the draft process, for guaranteed contracts, and for guaranteed league-wide minimum salaries. We fought for increased pre- and postseason pay, for player protection from injuries, for improved insurance and pension benefits. We fought for revisions in the standard option clause, for elimination of tolling and waivers. And we targeted and fought for players' rights in the wide range of issues regarding free agency.

I don't play anymore, but I have never really retired from the game. My mind and my heart are still in it, and I know from the other side of the fence how short the careers we worked so long for really are. Professional athletic careers are already over when the careers of other professionals start taking off. Doctors, lawyers, accountants, entertainers, they can do what they have prepared for until they are in their sixties. For 40 years, we have, on the average, only five. That makes a difference. If we don't establish our financial security before we leave the game, then, in far too many cases, our futures are all behind us. Ten years from now, the owners will still be owners, making more and more money. Ten years from now, members of the fourth estate will still be writing. But the players will be working, or looking for work, in some other occupation, usually one for which they had no time to prepare during their college days, during those days when they were preparing to be professional athletes. And, if we were good enough to make it, if we were good enough to make millions each year for the owners, then our services must be justly compensated.

Research is increasingly revealing that most professional football players have shorter life spans than the average adult male. Most of us suffer the rest of our lives from some injury sustained in the game. I say to the owners, make it worth it to us and we'll make being an owner worth even more to you.

Now I know that a lot of owners have the attitude that there are more where you fellows came from, that there are thousands of young men who want desperately to play football, to become famous and make your salaries. That's true, but will they be the best? Will there be that drive among the young athletes tomorrow who know the injury statistics, who know about life after football for those who do not come out financially secure, who know the work and the discipline and often the abandonment of academic careers—will there be that drive among the ever-more savvy players of tomorrow to keep the game as exciting to people around the world as it is today?

Will the owners of football teams make the same mistake that so many other owners of industry have made in recent years, thinking they don't have to pay for the best, that they can get by with an approximation of quality from others? Well, let me tell you, they won't find tight ends and tackles in Taiwan.

I'm not a player anymore, and I'm not here to suggest actions to you. I am only here to share with you the experiences of those who have gone before you. You, the players today, your player representatives, and your president must decide what is right for you now. This is your day.

The main things that I want to leave with you are the questions I posed in the beginning—Do you know who you are? Do you know what you want? Are you willing to fight to get it? Are you as competitive in the game of life as you are on the field? Because that is what this is all about— the game of life and the rest of your lives. If you decide at this conference that you are deter- mined to be the best you can be and have the best you can have for the rest of your lives, then let me say this in closing—get a game plan, get organized, get excited, and get started. If you do, you will feel the way I felt in Super Bowl V, when I reached up my hands for that winning pass. I knew it was coming. I knew it was my turn. I knew I would score. And that victory would belong to my team.

I don't know if the words I spoke were taken to heart. But I've always felt an obligation to the players that have come after me, as well as the ones I've played with, to be there for them if they needed the special knowledge and experience I had in labor matters with the NFL. I have always been there for my teammates, on and off the field.

It has been a long way from that first battle I led in 1970, and both sides have made some mistakes along the way. But the association and the owners have reached what is probably the most amicable working agreement of any major sport, and many observers have said that it was my free agency lawsuit that eventually paved the way for the labor relationship that now exists between players and owners—one that has made the NFL the success it is today.

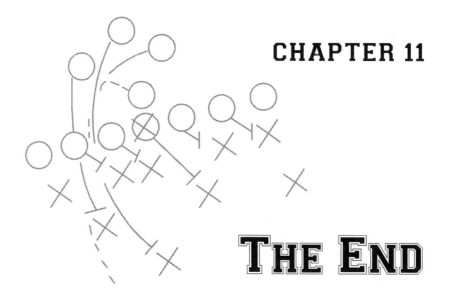

CHAPTER 11

THE END

Things seemed to be going well after we won the Super Bowl. Owner Carroll Rosenbloom threw us a big party and took all the players to the Bahamas. My role in the union was much calmer now compared to the strike we'd had the previous summer. And I had just been voted the greatest tight end in the first 50 years of the NFL.

The good times ended for me, though, just before we reported to camp in late July. I got a call from coach Don McCafferty. "I don't know how to tell you this, John, but I can't play you anymore," he said.

"What do you mean, you can't play me anymore?" I shot back. My knee was still hurting, but on one leg the season before, I was still third on the team in receptions. I could play.

"You're injured," McCafferty said.

"Where am I injured?" I asked.

"Your elbow," he said.

"Which one?" I asked.

"It doesn't matter, just tape one," he said.

And that was how the season would be for me. I was being punished for leading the Players Association. Tom Mitchell played tight end most of the time and led the team with 33 catches for 402 yards, a 12.2 yard-per-catch average. It was fewer yards than I had gotten on one leg the year before. I caught just 11 passes for 143 yards, a 13 yard-per-catch average, and no touchdowns. Johnny Unitas completed 92 of 176 passes for 942 yards, with just three touchdowns and nine interceptions. Earl Morrall connected on 84 of 167 passes for 1,210 yards, with seven touchdown passes and 12 interceptions.

But somehow we managed to go 10–4 and make the playoffs. We defeated the Cleveland Browns in the first round, 20–3, and went on to the AFC title game on January 2, 1972, this time against Don Shula and his up-and-coming Miami Dolphins, the Eastern Conference champions. With Bob Griese at quarterback, Larry Csonka (an old Syracuse runner) and Jim Kiick in the backfield, and Paul Warfield at wide receiver, Shula had an all-star offense and a "no-name" defense. They were coming off a remarkable win, having defeated the Kansas City Chiefs 27–24 on Christmas Day in a game that lasted six quarters—82 minutes and 40 seconds of play.

The game against Miami was a disaster. The Dolphins handled us on both sides of the ball, sending us home with a 21–0 loss. The magic wasn't there for Jim O'Brien this time. He missed two field goals, 46- and 48-yarders, and also had a 35-

yard attempt blocked by Miami defensive back Lloyd Mumford. But the turning point in the game came in the second period, when we had fourth and one inside the 10-yard line and the Dolphins stopped Don Nottingham. They hit us with two big plays—a 75-yard touchdown from Griese to Warfield in the first quarter and a pass interception by Dick Anderson returned 62 yards for a touchdown in the third quarter. They finished us off in the fourth quarter on a five-yard run by Csonka.

This would be the end of the Baltimore Colts as we knew them. The end of an era that began with Unitas 15 years earlier, the one I came upon in 1963. It would be the end for me as well. After the season I went to Rosenbloom and said, "I'll never play for you again as long as I live. You want to punish me? Well, you did. But you punished yourself as well. You could have gone to the Super Bowl again. What's the matter, did the other owners force you to promise to punish me this year? Did Pete Rozelle give you an order to bench me?"

Not long after that, Rosenbloom pulled off a bizarre deal with a Chicago businessman by the name of Robert Irsay, who had purchased the Los Angeles Rams as a prelude to this whole scheme. Rosenbloom was tired of Baltimore. He was frustrated about his failed attempts to get a new stadium and was also unhappy about the inability to draw large crowds for preseason games, when owners had a chance to make large sums of money. Rosenbloom wanted to get out to the good life in L.A. So on July 26, Irsay and Rosenbloom swapped franchises, and Baltimore definitely got the short end of the stick.

Irsay brought in a general manager named Joe Thomas, a former Colts line coach who had helped build the Miami

Dolphins' roster as personnel director but left after he lost a power struggle to gain more control over the organization. He was a ruthless, cold-hearted man with a personality that Dale Carnegie would hate. Not long after they took over, they began their effort to tear the team apart, and their tools were deceit and lies.

I was driving one day and heard on the radio that I had retired. Of course, I hadn't retired, and I sent a telegram to Pete Rozelle to tell him so. I had guaranteed money. I never asked for a no-cut clause. I didn't care if they cut me, but I cared if they paid me. They could send me to Egypt as long as I had guaranteed money, and I did—a five-year contract. Not five one-year contracts. It was one five-year contract, but I wasn't going out to play until my situation was cleared up.

When I heard the news, Irsay and Thomas were out of town. Thomas came back, and he called a meeting with me, McCafferty, Ernie Accorsi (the publicity director who would later become general manager), and Dick Bielski. I walked into the room, and Thomas had all the lights out. He had a chair placed in front of his desk. There was a single light shining on the chair. I walked into this setup and Thomas said, "You better get your ass out on that field, or I'll have you in court so fast your head will swim!"

I turned my back to him and said to McCafferty, Accorsi, and Bielski, "Hi Dick. Hi Coach. Hi Ernie. I'm going to pretend that this didn't really happen. I'm going to go back outside and knock on the door again. When I come back in, tell him he can't talk to me that way. Then we'll have some meaningful dialogue." So I walked out and knocked on the door again. I came in and said hello to everyone else in the room and sat down.

"You said you quit," Thomas said. "Tell me about it. Did you quit?" He was referring to a conversation I had with McCafferty, who had asked me several times if I was quitting, and I didn't give him an answer either way. I certainly did not say yes.

I shook my head no.

"Answer me," Thomas said. "I asked you a question."

I shook my head no again.

Thomas turned to McCafferty and said, "He just called you a liar."

"John, why did you call me a liar?" McCafferty asked me.

"Coach, how long have I known you?" I asked McCafferty. "Nine years? There's no way that I would call you a liar."

I pointed to Thomas and said, "Don't let him come between you and me. I have respect for you. None for him."

I started listing all the things I had told him. "Did this happen, did this happen?" McCafferty agreed with everything I said, so I replied, "Then where did I lie?"

"You didn't lie," McCafferty said. I knew it cost McCafferty something to say that, but he was a man and not Thomas' flunky. While this was going on, Thomas was getting more agitated. I looked over at him as he reached into his desk and pulled out some kind of white pill.

"No, no, no," I yelled. "I am not going to sit here and be subjected to drug abuse."

So I turned around to leave, and Thomas was beside himself with anger. He was screaming at me, "Don't you leave! Don't you leave!"

I thought maybe I could get him to pop a blood vessel or something. "I'm leaving now, Joe," I said. "I know you don't want me to see you like this."

I had been through all of these mind games with the owners and knew how they tried to intimidate players. There was nothing he could show me that I hadn't seen, and I knew he wouldn't expect a player to be able to throw it right back in his face. I had no respect for him, and he knew it.

That night, on the late news, I learned that I had been put on waivers. They would still have to pay me, although Thomas threatened to try to avoid it. He once said to me, "You'll get your money in the year 2000."

I wasn't going to take that from a minor leaguer like Joe Thomas. I called Rozelle and told him that I had a signed contract, and the Colts would have to pay me.

While this was going on, I had been picked up on waivers by the San Diego Chargers, but I had not reported. So I was getting calls from San Diego wanting to know where I was. Willie Wood, the former Packers safety who was now an assistant coach with the Chargers, called and asked, "Mack, what happened?"

"What do you mean, what happened?" I answered back.

"We're looking for you here," Wood said. "Harland [Svare, the Chargers head coach] is looking for you."

"You got my damned number," I said. "Why doesn't he call me?"

"I'll call him right now," Wood said. "Will you talk to Harland?"

I said I would, and then Svare called me. "I've got all the bad boys here," he said, referring to the veteran malcontents—such as linebacker Tim Rossovich, known for setting his hair on fire and eating broken glass—that Svare was bringing to San Diego. They were known as "Harland's Hoodlums."

"Well, I'm not a bad boy," I replied.

"Never mind that," he said. "Do you want to come out here?"

"I'm getting paid here," I said. "I have no incentive to come out there. I'm getting paid now for sitting at home."

Svare seemed like he was not going to take no for an answer, but I was prepared to say no in every way I could think of.

"I know there's more football in you," he said. "Why don't you come out here?"

I told him to call me back. I was thinking to myself, "I don't really want to go. I've played all my life in Baltimore. I know I'm going to get paid, so I'm going to stay home and think about what I want to do next."

Svare called me back and said, "We'll give you the same money you had in Baltimore."

"Where's my incentive?" I asked. "I'm going to get the money anyway."

"What will it take to get you to come?" he asked.

"Double my salary," I said.

"What?" Svare said.

"Double my salary," I said again.

"OK," Svare said. "What else do you want?"

"I can't come unless I bring my wife and kids," I said. "I've always had my wife and kids with me."

"OK, bring your wife and kids and your housekeeper if you want," Svare said.

"I don't have a housekeeper," I said.

"What else will it take?" Svare said.

"I need three cars," I said.

"Three cars?" Svare asked.

"One for me, one for my wife, and one for the housekeeper," I said.

"You got it," Svare said.

This was getting crazy. I was trying to invent impossible demands, but I ran out of things to ask for, and Svare won. I agreed to report. It was a huge mistake.

In Baltimore the equipment manager had always taken pride in our appearance. So that was what I expected when I arrived in San Diego. I told the equipment manager in San Diego, "Hey, I'm John Mackey, and I'm reporting from the world champion Baltimore Colts. I like my shoes shined, my helmet cleaned and polished and sprayed, and my practice uniform pressed. I play the way I look."

This was his response: "Here's the shoe polish for your shoes. Here's the cleaner for your helmet and the spray. I put your jocks, T-shirts, and socks in a pile, and if you get here early, you might get your size."

It was a completely different attitude. Little things that never would have happened in Baltimore, like a rookie missing the warm-up because he was trying to scalp his tickets out in front of the stadium and got arrested by the police, were glossed over. If that had happened in Baltimore, Shula would have run him out of the whole world. But nothing happened to him in San Diego. They slapped him on the wrist and said, "Don't ever do that again." Svare yelled at him, "What kind of stupid idea is this? What kind of team do we have here?" Then the kid got dressed and played.

Svare was a piece of work. He had played linebacker for the New York Giants in the fifties and went into coaching at a young age. When he was 31 he became the youngest head coach in the NFL when he was hired to coach the Rams with six weeks left in the 1962 season, but he failed miserably and was fired in the middle of the 1965 season with a 14–31–3 record. He was replaced by George Allen.

Svare would say things like, "I know we're not going to win, but we owe it to our fans to look good while we're losing." I listened to this in disbelief. In all my years of football, I had never heard a coach say something like that. I thought to myself, "If you know we're not going to win, what the hell are we going out there for?"

It was a different type of organization. We had some outstanding players, in terms of individual talent, but it was so disorganized. We practiced early in the morning, which didn't make sense because our games were at 1:00 in the afternoon. I never could understand why we didn't practice when we would play so that at least we would have the knowledge of how the sun came into this stadium at that time, and other things that could affect our play. We would practice, come in for lunch, then go back to watch game films or go over game plans, and then go home. I asked Svare why we came in so early, and he said, "I want to make this as much a 9-to-5 job as I can."

In Baltimore it was just the opposite. We came in at noon and had our meeting, looked at films, and then discussed what we were going to do on the field. We went on the field to practice at 2:00 P.M. because we usually played at 2:00 P.M. We knew how the sun would affect our vision, or how the winds might act at that time.

We didn't have a two-minute drill in San Diego, which I couldn't believe. I asked Svare, "Where's our two-minute drill?"

and he said, "Just do what you did in Baltimore." It was a completely different system, though. Their system was that the pass receiver ran the pattern called in the huddle, and adjustments were made by the quarterback based on what he saw and what the defense was giving. The receivers were not allowed to read defenses or make adjustments. But in Baltimore, everyone read defenses and everyone made adjustments. Not only did you make the adjustment, if your teammate made a mistake and ran the wrong pattern, you adjusted to him. It was up to Unitas to read what was happening downfield and he would find the man who was open. You could have a play that started out busted, but we capitalized on it, and if it worked, they might put it in the game plan for the next time. We were always talking and communicating. A lot of plays were discovered because a mistake was made and we adjusted to it and somehow were able to salvage the play when Unitas read it.

The problem for me in San Diego was that I was not allowed to do that. When Unitas wound up being traded to San Diego, I came back for another season because I knew that with John I could make all of those different adjustments because John could read them. At least I could have if John was playing, but his San Diego experience was just as bizarre as mine. We both had problems with the coaching staff. There was one assistant coach, Bob Schnelker, a former tight end with the Giants and Packers. We called him Colonel Klink, like the character from the television show *Hogan's Heroes*. He seemed to resent the Colts system we brought with us and the success we had back in Baltimore. Here's an example from a scrimmage of the way they did business: One play had the two backs go away from the tight end on a passing situation, but if the strong side linebacker blitzes, there's no one to pick him up. The two backs flare the other way. If the quarterback is right-handed, as he takes the ball and comes back in a right formation, he can see that linebacker and he can drop the ball off. But if he's in a left formation and the two halfbacks are playing to the right, and he's a right-handed quarterback, when he pulls out he has his back to the strong side. He can't see. I was always taught that whenever that happens, I should check the linebacker before running the pattern. If the linebacker comes, you take him out to protect the quarterback's blind side. I did it in this scrimmage, and Schnelker said to me, "We were in the right formation. Why didn't you release?"

"The linebacker started to blitz and I checked him, and when he came, I took him," I said.

"You just do what you're told," he told me.

You can't stand there and argue with the guy, explaining the play, because then the coach resents the implication that you know more than he does. So I just thought to hell with it and kept my mouth shut. We ran it again, and this time a rookie quarterback was in there, and he got nailed. He dropped back, flared the backs the other way, and the linebacker struck him from the blind side. Here was a player who could have gotten hurt, and I wanted to kick Schnelker's ass after that. Shula had learned to communicate with players about football and would listen to what you had to say.

Svare was no better than Schnelker. He used to stand at practice, his hands clasped behind his back, just looking up at the sky. After a half hour or so, the whole team would be doing the same thing, trying to see what Harland saw. It was embarrassing to be part of that team.

The further you got into the organization, the worse things got. The Chargers were in the middle of a huge drug scandal in the early seventies, and I saw it firsthand. When I got to San Diego, I noticed that before games a lot of players were getting little white envelopes. I wasn't getting one, so I went to Svare and asked him where mine was. "You've got to talk to Dr. Mandell," Svare said, referring to Arnold Mandell, the team doctor. So I went to see him.

"Doc, where's my white envelope?" I asked. "You think that because I'm president of the Players Association that you're going to treat me differently?" After all I had gone through by this point in my career, I was a little paranoid about my position and the football decisions made around me.

"You don't need them," he said. "I've been studying you, and you don't need this."

I found out there were drugs—amphetamines, uppers and downers, and the like—in those little white envelopes.

"Today's college football players and the new guys coming in have been smoking so much grass, they are coming in too placid," Mandell said. "So I give them a little something to get them going, with a booster at halftime. And because the first pill gives them problems with sex, I give them this other one to keep their wives and girlfriends happy." I couldn't believe this man.

He gave a talk using a blackboard that was incredible. "Let me tell you something," he said, drawing a graph on the board. "We're getting kids from college who smoke a lot of marijuana. This is a violent game that requires emotion. This line is the line that separates the great from the mediocre. If you want to be a great player, all your ups and downs must be above this line. If you want to be an average player, your ups and downs must be around the line. Now, I give you an amphetamine, I can't take you from here [pointing to the average line] to superstar. But if I can get you to move up about 15 percent, I can get you up over that line. But I can't take a mediocre or average player and make him a superstar." Eventually, the San Diego drug mess would become public. The NFL fined the Chargers $20,000 and Svare $5,000, and eight players were fined between $1,000 and $3,000 each.

It was one circus after another in San Diego, which made it prime territory for someone like Duane Thomas, the talented but troubled Cowboys running back. Thomas had been traded to the Chargers in July 1972, but he showed up just a few times for brief moments during training camp and then disappeared. We played the first seven games of the season without him, and then he suddenly showed up acting as if he was ready to play. Of course, the team we were playing that week was the Dallas Cowboys.

Thomas had not even practiced with us. But Svare had him dress in the locker room before the game, and it appeared that he would play. We went out on the field to do warm-ups. After several exercises, Deacon Jones told me to look downfield under the goal posts. There was Thomas, sitting under the goal posts in a yoga-like position, watching the Cowboys going through their warm-ups. He wasn't moving. He just sat there, staring. And he stayed there staring when we went back to the locker room to put on our game equipment, and he was still there when we returned for the opening kickoff. He was literally dragged off the field by security while the national anthem was playing. That was the end of the Duane Thomas era in San Diego.

I wouldn't be long for San Diego either. I finished the season having caught just 11 passes for 110 yards in 13 games for no touchdowns. I would come back the following season when John Unitas got traded to the Chargers, but it was not the same. It was not Baltimore for either of us.

By the end of my football career, I had 331 catches in 139 games for 5,236 yards—a 15.8 yard-per-catch average—and 38 touchdowns. I'd like to think that I gave as good as I got in the game, that I had contributed as much as I had received from football. A long time before, my mother had asked that if I was going to play football, be the best football player I could be. I listened to my mother.

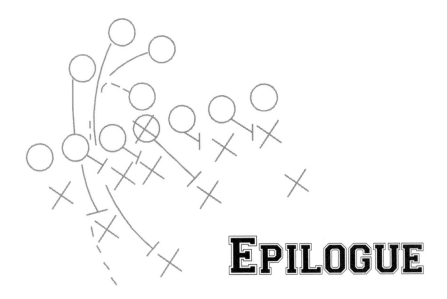

EPILOGUE

It has been a good life for me away from the football field. It seemed that I was destined for something more than simply being a football player, although, make no mistake about it, I am very proud of what I accomplished on the field. I was very blessed to have played with some of the greatest teammates a man could ever have known, and I wouldn't trade my time in the National Football League for any other era—even today's times, when players make so much more money. I know this sounds strange coming from a man who fought so hard for a piece of the lucrative revenue pie, but there was a price to pay for the success the players have had since the days when I led the Players Association. The money has certainly changed the game and has changed the players as well. Perhaps that was inevitable.

It is still a great game, though. People think that because of the battles I fought as a union leader with the owners, and then in my lawsuit to become a free agent, that I hated the NFL. Nothing could be further from the truth. I just had an overriding sense of justice, having grown up in a home where respect for everyone was drilled into us, and I knew in my heart that what was right and good for everyone in the league was to have a more fair and equitable system for the players than what was in place when I played the game. I knew that down the road the game could be destroyed by the bad feelings on both sides. And it nearly did tear the game apart in the eighties. But through court decisions—the groundwork for which was laid by my battle for free agency 20 years earlier—and leadership on both sides, they have come up with a system that allows players to be free agents and, unlike baseball, not bankrupt the teams.

After I left the game, I was involved in a number of different business ventures, some successful and some not. I was a player's agent for a while, and I did my share of public speaking and motivational talks. I was involved in numerous community and charitable activities and also did political work for my good friend and old union colleague, former Congressman Jack Kemp. And I was always a consultant and confidant to the union, offering my expertise to try to guide them through the tough times. Sometimes they listened, other times they did not. I also became more involved with the league that I had battled against so hard as a player, particularly when Paul Tagliabue took over as commissioner. He was a man who I felt had a sense of justice and fairness, and I was glad to help whenever I was called upon to be part of some kind of league activity or event.

I've been president of my own company and helped run other firms. I've served as chairman of the National Board of Advisors of the Community for Education Foundation and its Overcoming Obstacles life skills instruction and employment opportunities program for our nation's youth. I've been on the board of advisors to the Leukemia Society of America, the board of advisors of the Syracuse University Business School, the board of directors for the Syracuse Alumni Association, the International Advisory Committee for the Harlem Globetrotters, and the board of advisors for Empower America. I've also worked for the Better Boys Foundation in Chicago and its annual sports banquet, the Mackey Awards, named after me. I've received numerous honors including the Paul Robeson Award for Community Involvement from the NAACP, Man of the Year from the NFL Players Association, and the Ernie Davis Award from the Leukemia Society of America.

Through all of it, I always treasured the life at home that my wife, Sylvia, had created for our family. She is so much a part of me—my heart, soul, and conscience—and is an intelligent (a graduate of Syracuse University and a linguist who could speak French and Russian) and honest woman, who is every bit the role model that people would say that I was. And, if I may say so, a beautiful woman who has worked as an actress and model both in Europe and the United States. She raised three wonderful children—Lisa, Kevin, and Laura—all of whom graduated from college and went on to build their own lives. Lisa graduated from Howard University and has a master's degree in education from that school. As an elementary school reading specialist, she is helping young children learn the joys of reading, and she is married and raising two great boys, Ben and Joe, both of whom are playing football. Ben, in fact, is a tight end and wore number 88 for his local Boys and Girls Club team. Kevin graduated from the University of California at Berkeley and is a civil engineer. He is also raising three wonderful girls, Vanessa, Sabrina, and Anna Sophia. He is a football coach as well—an offensive and defensive line coach in Pop Warner football, teaching seven-, eight-, and nine-year-old kids. I did manage to convince my youngest, Laura, to go to my alma mater, Syracuse, where she received a degree in English literature. She has worked in the fashion and retail industry and has traveled and studied in places like London, Florence, Cairo, and Hong Kong. I am so proud of all of them. They have given me so much joy. I'd like to think I left a legacy behind for them to be proud of as well.

In the fall of 2002, Syracuse University announced the John Mackey Football Scholarship. Back in my hometown on Long Island, they have the John Mackey Award, presented by the Nassau County Sports Commission and awarded annually to the most outstanding tight end in Division 1-A college football. And, finally, I have taken my place alongside the greats of the game in the Pro Football Hall of Fame.

My name has often been mentioned, along with the likes of Curt Flood and Muhammad Ali, as a pioneer in both sports and society in the sixties and seventies through my role as a union leader. It wasn't a role I sought, and I leave it to others to decide my place in the history of sports in America in the 20th century. But let me leave it at this: I am the son of my father, a man who had only love in his heart even when facing a world full of hatred, a man who believed in the good in people. I hope that I have carried on that legacy. In the end, it is the best that a man can leave behind.

INDEX

209

Mackey with, 52, 56–110, 147–68
and Mackey's Hall of Fame
   induction, 1–18
Mackey's last season with,
   192–93, 194–96
and Mackey's Players Association
   presidency, 3, 4–5, 8, 61,
   139–40, 142, 144–46, 170–90,
   191, 192
McCafferty as coach of, 161, 166,
   167, 191–92, 194, 195
on *Monday Night Football*, 162
1958 and 1959 NFL championship
   wins over Giants, 58, 105
1963 season, 63–87
1964 season, 89–94, 96–101, 108
1965 season, 103–6, 108
1966 season, 106–10
1967 season, 151–52
1968 NFL championship, 64
1968 season, 152–54
1969 season, 159–60
1970 season, 161–68, 179
1971 season, 192
in 1972 AFC title game, 192–93
Parker on being drafted by, 131
Parker on Colts owner Carroll
   Rosenbloom, 136–38
Parker's rookie season with,
   compared to Mackey's, 131–33
racism and segregation issues
   within, 133–35, 147–48
Shula's departure as coach of, 160,
   161
and *Sports Illustrated* controversy,
   140–41
in Super Bowl III, vs. Jets, 64,
   157–59, 163
Super Bowl V victory, vs.
   Cowboys, 164–68
Unitas on departure of the Colts
   from Baltimore, 113
in Western Conferences, 102–3,
   104–6
See also Shula, Don

Baltimore News American, 3
Baltimore News-Post, 72–77, 80–85
Baltimore Ravens, 7, 18
Baltimore Sun, 3, 57
Barney, Lem, 6, 7
baseball, 25, 47
basketball, 25–26, 47
Bell, Bert, 58, 139–40
Bell, Bob, 34
Bennett & Owens (sports
   management firm), 142
Berry, Raymond, 5, 57, 63, 66, 70,
   86, 92, 93–94, 100, 101, 103,
   106, 119, 128, 132
Bielski, Dick, 194
Biletnikoff, Fred, 163
Blanda, George, 163, 164
blocking, 43–44, 47, 97, 124–25, 143
Boston Patriots, 161, 162
bowl games, 41, 45, 46, 48, 86, 87,
   109, 111, 128, 140
Boyd, Bob, 159, 161
Braase, Ordell, 152, 161, 169
Bratkowski, Zeke, 105–6
Brickman, Alan, 3–4, 57, 60, 61, 62
Brown, Bill, 156
Brown, Ed, 104
Brown, Jim, 29, 33, 42, 43, 47, 48,
   52, 102, 103, 115, 130
Brown, John, 38–39, 48, 52
Brown, Paul, 50, 103
Brown, Roger, 133
Buffalo Bills, 1, 8, 122, 161, 162,
   170
Bulaich, Norm, 163, 164, 166
Butkus, Dick, 94, 98–99, 109, 136

Camp Concern, 150–51
Canadian Football League, 131
Canton Bulldogs, 5
Canton, Ohio, Hall of Fame
   ceremonies in, 5–17
Carey, Max, 120
Chandler, Don, 105
Chicago Bears, 69, 132